孔子学院总部赠送
Donated by Confucius Institute Headquarters

【中国圣人文化丛书】

孟子
精华版

A Selected Collection of Mencius

编注：蔡希勤
英译：何祚康

华语教学出版社
SINOLINGUA

First Edition 2006
Second Printing 2007

ISBN 978-7-80200-219-7
Copyright 2006 by Sinolingua
Published by Sinolingua
24 Baiwanzhuang Road, Beijing 100037, China
Tel: (86) 10-68320585
Fax: (86) 10-68326333
http//: www. sinolingua.com.cn
E-mail:hyjx@ sinolingua.com.cn
Printed by Beijing Foreign Languages Printing House
Distributed by China International
Book Trading Corporation
35 Chegongzhuang Xilu, P.O. Box 399
Beijing 100044, China

Printed in the People's Republic of China

前　言

　　孟子（约公元前372——前289年）名轲，字子舆，邹（今山东省邹县）人，中国战国时期的大儒，孔子后一人，有"亚圣"之称。他幼时曾得力于母亲的教诲，后受业于子思的门人。游学于齐、梁之间，一度任齐宣王客卿，因其主张不见用，退而与弟子公孙丑、万章等著书立说。适应历史发展的需要，孟子发展孔子核心思想仁为仁政，提出"民贵君轻"说，体现了儒家的重民思想，反对统治者的武力兼并，主张"仁政"是统一天下的基础。孟子提倡性善说，在中国思想史上具有重要意义。孟子强调养心、存心等内心修养的功夫，成为中国思想史上心学的鼻祖。

　　宋元以后，孟子学说成为统治阶级的重要精神支柱之一，其本人的地位也日益显尊，元至顺元年（公元1330年），封为邹国亚圣公，明嘉靖九年（公元1530年）定为"亚圣孟子"。

所著《孟子》七篇，是中国儒家经典之一，与《大学》、《中庸》、《论语》并称《四书》。书中记载了孟子及其若干弟子的政治、教育、哲学、伦理等各方面的思想观点和政治活动规迹，是研究儒家学说及其发展的重要典籍，也是了解孟子本人及其学派的重要依据与资料。

为了帮助青年读者能够读懂这部儒家经典，前几年华语教学出版社以文白、汉英对照版和《大学》、《论语》、《中庸》一起出版。向海内外发行，受到广大读者的关注。

现在作为"中国圣人文化丛书"之一的《孟子》精华版，对原有篇章有所删减，又增加了一些注释和精美插图，使本书更具观赏性和实用价值。

PREFACE

Mencius (c. 372 – 289 BC) was a native of the minor State of Zou (now Zouxian County, Shandong Province). His personal name was Ke and courtesy name Ziyu. He was the outstanding Confucian sage of the Warring States Period (475 – 221 BC). He received instruction first from his mother and later from a pupil of Zisi, a grandson of Confucius. He traveled and taught in the states of Liang and Qi, being employed as a "guest minister" by King Huan of the latter state. But, disappointed that his political and philosophical ideas were not put into practice by his master, he retired to teach his disciples and write books.

Mencius developed the idea of benevolence, a key theme of Confucius' doctrines, and extended it to encompass benevolent government. Such a political system, he maintained, would be the foundation for the unification of the world. Like Confucius, he championed justice for the people above the might and right of rulers, and deplored the practice—all too common at the time—of states annexing each other by force. His theory that man is naturally good occupies a significant position in the history of Chinese thought. He stressed that goodness was the result of the "cultivation of the heart".

During the Song (960 – 1279) and Yuan (1271 – 1368) dynasties Mencius' teachings were absorbed as the mainstay of ruling class ideology. In 1330 he was awarded the exalted title of "Lesser Sage of the State of Zou", and in 1530 accorded the title "Mencius, the Lesser Sage".

The seven chapters of the *Mencius* comprise one of the classics of the Confucian school, and, together with *The Great Learn-*

ing, *The Doctrine of the Mean* and *Analects of Confucius*, one of the "Four Books". There are various opinions as to the compilation of the *Mencius*. One theory has it that it was composed by Mencius himself with the assistance of his disciples, chief of whom were Wan Zhang and Gongsun Chou; another theory is that it is simply a collection of the sage's sayings compiled after his death by his disciples and their pupils.

In the book are recorded the views of Mencius and his disciples on politics, education, philosophy and ethics, as well as accounts of some of their doings. It is an important document for the study of the Confucian School and its development, and essential reading for an understanding of Mencius and his doctrines.

To help young readers understand this great Chinese classic, a translation into the modern vernacular is appended, passage by passage, as is a version in English for the benefit of readers abroad.

目 录

《孟子》和《论语》一样本无篇名,是后人选每篇第一章的前几个重要的字而命名的。

前言

一、梁惠王上篇 …………………（1）
二、梁惠王下篇 …………………（19）
三、公孙丑上篇 …………………（42）
四、公孙丑下篇 …………………（61）
五、滕文公上篇 …………………（70）
六、滕文公下篇 …………………（78）
七、离娄上篇 ……………………（88）
八、离娄下篇 ……………………（122）
九、万章上篇 ……………………（145）
十、万章下篇 ……………………（154）
十一、告子上篇 …………………（162）
十二、告子下篇 …………………（192）
十三、尽心上篇 …………………（202）
十四、尽心下篇 …………………（227）

Contents

Preface

1. King Hui of Liang, Part One ······ (1)
2. King Hui of Liang, Part Two ······ (19)
3. Gongsun Chou, Part One ········ (42)
4. Gongsun Chou, Part Two ········ (61)
5. Duke Wen of Teng, Part One ··· (70)
6. Duke Wen of Teng, Part Two ··· (78)
7. Li Lou, Part One ················ (88)
8. Li Lou, Part Two ················ (122)
9. Wan Zhang, Part One ············ (145)
10. Wan Zhang, Part Two ·········· (154)
11. Gao Zi, Part One ··············· (162)
12. Gao Zi, Part Two ··············· (192)
13. Jin Xin, Part One ··············· (202)
14. Jin Xin, Part Two ··············· (227)

Note: The chapters of the *Mencius*, like those of the *Analects of Confucius*, were originally not titled, but were later given titles using key words that appeared at the beginning of each.

◎ 目录 CONTENTS

一、梁惠王上篇
King Hui of Liang, Part One

《孟子》之首篇。孟子初见梁惠王、齐宣王,讲自己"仁者无敌"的政治主张。本篇共7章,节选其中6章。

梁惠王对孟子说:"当初魏国比任何国家都强大,可是现在东边败给齐国,连太子也战死了;西边又败给秦国,丧失了河西之地七百余里;南边又被楚国掠去八座城池。我知道这是奇耻大辱,请您告诉我怎样才能报仇雪恨,使魏国强大起来?"孟子说:"你如果对人民实行仁政,减免刑罚,减轻赋税,让老百姓安居乐业,使年轻人受到教育,就能使魏国强大起来。这就是说'仁者无敌',你不要怀疑。"

1.1 孟子见梁惠王。王曰："叟！不远千里而来，亦将有以利吾国乎？"孟子对曰："王！何必曰利？亦有仁义而已矣。王曰，'何以利吾国？'大夫曰，'何以利吾家？'士庶人曰，'何以利吾身？'上下交征利而国危矣。万乘之国，弑其君者，必千乘之家；千乘之国，弑其君者，必百乘之家。万取千焉，千取百焉，不为不多矣。苟为后义而先利，不夺不餍。未有仁而遗其亲者也，未有义而后其君者也。王亦曰仁义而已矣，何必曰利？"

《梁惠王上篇·1》

梁惠王：即魏惠王，名莹（yīng）。公元前370年即位。公元前362年，因畏秦兵将国都由安邑（今山西省安邑县）迁至大梁（今河南省开封市），故魏又称梁。

Mencius had an audience with King Hui of Liang. The King said, "Venerable sir, you have made a very long journey to come and see me. Therefore, I take it that you have some suggestion for profiting my kingdom."

Mencius replied, "Why must Your Highness mention profit? What I have to suggest is benevolence and justice, and nothing more. If Your Highness says, 'How can I profit my kingdom?' the officials will say, 'How can we profit our families?' and the squires and the common people will say, 'How can we profit ourselves?' If superiors and inferiors contend among themselves for profit, the state will be endangered. In a kingdom of ten thousand chariots the person who assassinates its ruler must be the head of a household of one thousand chariots; in a kingdom of one thousand chariots the person who assassinates its ruler must be the head of a household of one hundred chariots. The number of chariots possessed by the families who kill the kings is not small. But if they treasure profit more than justice, they will never be satisfied until they have usurped all the property of the kings. It never happens that a humane person abandons his parents or that a just man repudiates his sovereign. Let Your Highness then talk only of benevolence and justice. Why must you talk of profit?"

Note: King Hui of Liang was also called King Hui of Wei. His original name was Ying and he ascended the throne in 370 BC. In 362 BC he moved his capital from Anyi (now Anyi County, Shanxi Province) to Daliang (now Kaifeng, Henan Province).

孟子谒见梁惠王。惠王说:"老丈!您不远千里而来,莫不是对我的国家带来了什么利益吧?"

孟子答道:"王,您何必要说什么利呢?仁义才是最重要的呢。假如王说'怎样才对我的国家有利?'大夫说'怎样才对我的封地有利?'士子、百姓说'怎样才对我本人有利?'举国上下都去追逐利益,国家可就危险了。"

孟子说:"在拥有一万辆兵车的国家里,造反杀害国君的,只能是拥有千辆兵车的大夫。在拥有一千辆兵车的国家里,造反杀害国君的,只能是拥有百辆兵车的大夫。万乘之国,大夫拥有兵车千乘。千乘之国,大夫拥有兵车百乘,大夫拥有的不能说不多了。但是，如果上上下下都把利摆在前头，那大夫若不夺杀国君就不能满足其贪欲了。讲'仁'的人不会遗弃自己的父母兄弟，讲'义'的人不会把君主抛开不管。所以，您只讲'仁义'就行了，何必去说利呢？"

1.2　孟子见梁惠王。王立于沼上，顾鸿雁麋鹿，曰："贤者亦乐此乎？"孟子对曰："贤者而后乐此，不贤者虽有此，不乐也。诗云：'经始灵台，经之营之，庶民攻之，不日成之。经始勿亟，庶民子来。王在灵囿，麀鹿攸伏，麀鹿濯濯，白鸟鹤鹤。王在灵沼，于牣鱼跃。'文王以民力为台为沼，而民欢乐之，谓其台曰灵台，谓其沼曰灵沼，乐其有麋鹿鱼鳖。古之人与民偕乐，故能乐也。汤誓曰：'时日害丧，予及女偕亡。'民欲与之偕亡，虽有台池鸟兽，岂能独乐哉？"

《梁惠王上篇·2》

文王：周文王，周王朝的建立者。

Mencius found King Hui of Liang standing by a pond and looking at rare birds and animals. The king asked,"Do virtuous men enjoy these things also?" Mencius answered,"Only if a man is virtuous can he enjoy these things; a wicked man would not enjoy them even if he possessed them. The *Book of Songs* says,'When Ling Terrace was being built, it was soon finished as everyone pitched in. All the people put their best efforts into the job even though the king said that there was no need to hurry. When the king went to the deer park, the female deer were at ease. The deer were fat and the feathers of the white birds shone. When the king went to Ling Pond, all the fish in the pond jumped happily.' This means that when King Wen of Zhou mobilized the people to build the terrace and the pond, all the people did it in high spirit and called the platform Ling Terrace and the pond Ling Pond. All the people rejoiced at King Wen's having so many rare animals and birds, because in ancient times kings shared their enjoyment with the people. But Jie of Xia Dynasty did the opposite. He proclaimed himself the sun, but the people resented this and said, 'Sun, when will you perish? We would like to perish with you.' If a king should be hated by his people to such a degree, could he enjoy terraces, ponds, and rare animals and birds ?"

Note: King Wen was the founder of the Zhou Dynasty (c. 1100 – 221 BC).

孟子谒见梁惠王。王正站在池塘旁边一边欣赏着园子里的珍禽异兽,一边得意地对孟子说:"有道德的人也乐于享受这种快乐吗?"

孟子回答说:"只有有道德的人才能够享受到这种快乐,没有道德的人纵使有这种快乐也是享受不了的。《诗经·灵台篇》说:'开始筑灵台,经营复经营,大家齐努力,很快便完成。王说不用急,百姓更努力。王到鹿苑中,母鹿正安逸。母鹿光且肥,白鸟羽毛洁。王到灵沼上,满池鱼跳跃。'这是说周文王虽然动用民力修筑高台池沼,但老百姓却很高兴,把台叫做

'灵台'，把池叫做'灵沼'，老百姓高兴文王有那么多珍禽异兽，因为文王肯和百姓们一同享受这种快乐。夏桀却与此相反，他自比太阳，老百姓怨恨他，就说：'太阳呀！你什么时候消亡，我宁愿跟你一道死去！'做为一国之君，竟使百姓怨恨到这种地步，他纵然有高台深池，珍禽异兽，难道能独享其乐吗？"

1.3 梁惠王曰："寡人之于国也，尽心焉耳矣。河内凶，则移其民于河东，移其粟于河内。河东凶亦然。察邻国之政，无如寡人之用心者。邻国之民不加少，寡人之民不加多，何也？"孟子对曰："王好战，请以战喻。填然鼓之，兵刃既接，弃甲曳兵而走。或百步而后止，或五十步而后止。以五十步笑百步，则何如？"曰："不可；直不百步耳，是亦走也。"曰："王如知此，则无望民之多于邻国也。"

《梁惠王上篇·3》节选

河内、河东：魏国的河内地即指黄河北岸，今河南省济源县一带；河东地即指今山西省安邑县一带。

King Hui of Liang said to Mencius, "I pay great attention to the welfare of my kingdom. When the Henei area suffers natural disasters I move the people there to the Hedong area and feed them, and send grain to the Henei area to provide relief to the old, weak, sick and disabled. When the Hedong area suffers natural disasters I do the same. I have investigated the governments of the neighbouring kingdoms and found that no other king takes as much care of the people as I. Yet why do no people of the neighboring kingdoms come to my kingdom to seek refuge?"

Mencius answered, "Your Highness is fond of war, so let me explain by means of a martial metaphor. After the drums roll to start the advance the two armies clash. Suddenly the soldiers throw away their armor and run for their lives, trailing their weapons. Now, suppose that some of them stop after one hundred paces and some stop only after fifty paces. Is it right for those who stop after fifty paces to laugh at those who stop after one hundred paces for running so far away?"

The king said, "No. Just because they have not run as far as one hundred paces does not mean that they have not fled the same as the others."

Mencius said, "If Your Highness knows this, you should not expect the people of the neighboring kingdoms to seek refuge with you."

Note: Henei and Hedong: The Henei area refers to the north side of the Yellow River, approximately Jiyuan County in Henan Province; Hedong refers approximately to Anyi County in Shanxi Province.

梁惠王对孟子说："我对于国家，可算是尽心尽力了。河内地方遇到灾荒，我就把那里的人民迁移到河东就食，同时又把河东的粮食运到河内以救济那里的老弱病残。河东地方遇到灾荒我也这样办，我曾经考察过邻国的政治，没有一个国家的国君能像我这样替老百姓打算的。可是邻国的百姓却并没有来投奔我，这是什么缘故呢？"

孟子回答说："王喜好战争，我就以战争打个比喻吧。战端一开，两军刚一接战，兵士们就丢盔卸甲往后逃跑，有的一口气跑了一百步，有的跑了五十步。那些跑了五十步的兵士耻笑跑了一百步的兵士胆子小，跑那么远，这对不对呢？"

梁惠王说："不对，只不过他没有跑到一百步罢了，其实都是在逃跑，性质是一样的。"

孟子说："王如果懂得这个道理，那就不要希望邻国的百姓会归服于你了。"

1.4 孟子曰："庖有肥肉，厩有肥马，民有饥色，野有饿莩，此率兽而食人也。兽相食，且人恶之；为民父母，行政，不免于率兽而食人，恶在其为民父母也？"

《梁惠王上篇·4》节选

Mencius continued, "Now, Your Highness has more than enough meat in your kitchen and more than enough strong horses in your stables. But your people look hungry and there are people who are starving to death by the roadsides. This is tantamount to the men in power leading animals to devour human beings. How can such men be officials?"

孟子对梁惠王说:"您现在厨房里有吃不完的肉,马厩里有用不完健壮的马匹,可是老百姓却面有饥色,路上有饿死的人,这就等于执政者领着禽兽来吃人。人们对禽兽间的自相残食都感到厌恶,执政者却领着禽兽来吃人,这怎么能做老百姓的父母官呢?"

1.5 孟子曰:"地方百里而可以王。王如施仁政于民,省刑罚,薄税敛,深耕易耨;壮者以暇日修其孝悌忠信,入以事其父兄,出以事其长上,可使制梃以挞秦楚之坚甲利兵矣。彼夺其民时,使不得耕耨以养其父母。父母冻饿,兄弟妻子离散。彼陷溺其民,王往而征之,夫谁与王敌?故曰:'仁者无敌。'王请勿疑!"

《梁惠王上篇·5》节选

梃(tǐng):棍棒。仁者无敌:《孟子·离娄上》:"孔子曰：'仁不可为众也。夫国君好仁，天下无敌。'……'夫国君能好仁，则天下无敢与之敌也。'"孟子引孔子的话强调了统治者有德、施仁政的重要作用在于得民心，而民心的向背是政治上成功或失败的决定因素。

Mencius answered, "A small kingdom of one hundred *li* can make the world submit to it by practicing a policy of benevolence. If Your Highness could practice a policy of benevolence, mitigate punishments, reduce taxation, allow people to cultivate intensively, and educate youngsters in the principles of filial piety, respect for their elder brothers, and honesty and keeping one's word toward others so as to support and wait upon their parents and elder brothers at home and to respect their superiors when they themselves become officials, then you could resist the mighty armor and weapons of Qin and Chu with mere clubs. Since Qin and Chu conscript ceaselessly, the common people have no time to cultivate their land. Their parents consequently suffer from hunger and cold, and their brothers and wives are scattered. The kings of Qin and Chu cast their people into an abyss of misery. Will their people resist you when you send a punitive expedition against them? You should not doubt the truth of the saying that he who practices benevolence is invincible!"

孟子对梁惠王说："一个百里小国就可以实行仁政而使天下归服。您如果能对人民实行仁政，减免刑罚，减轻赋税，让老百姓精耕细作；还要使年轻人有机会学习，使他们懂得孝顺父母、敬爱兄长、对人忠诚守信的道理。他们用这些道理在家侍奉父兄，在朝为官便会尊敬上级。这样的话，就是用木棒也可以抗击秦、楚两国的坚甲利兵了。因为秦国和楚国无休止地征兵征工，老百姓没有时间耕种，田地荒芜，连父母也不能养活，他们的父母挨冻受饿，兄弟妻子背井离乡。秦王和楚王已使自己的百姓陷入水深火热之中，您去讨伐他，会有人抵抗您吗？所以说：'仁者无敌'的话是对的，您不要怀疑！"

1.7 齐宣王问曰："齐桓、晋文之事可得闻乎？"孟子对曰："仲尼之徒无道桓文之事者，是以后世无传焉，臣未之闻也。无以，则王乎？"曰："德何如则可以王矣？"曰："保民而王，莫之能御也。"……曰："挟太山以超北海，语人曰，'我不能。'是诚不能也。为长者折枝，语人曰，'我不能。'是不为也，非不能也。故王之不王，非挟太山以超北海之类也；王之不王，是折枝之类也。老吾老，以及人之老；幼吾幼，以及人之幼。天下可运于掌。诗云，'刑于寡妻，至于兄弟，以御于家邦。'言举斯心加诸彼而已。故推恩足以保四海，不推恩无以保妻子。"

《梁惠王上篇·7》节选

齐宣王：齐国国君。齐威王之子，姓田，名辟疆。其祖先为春秋时姜姓齐国的大夫，后夺齐国政权。齐宣王是田氏齐国第四代国君。**齐桓、晋文**：齐桓公，名小白；晋文公，名重耳，在春秋时期先后称霸于诸侯。齐宣王也想称霸诸侯，统一天下，所以向孟子了解"齐桓、晋文之事"。

King Xuan of Qi asked Mencius: "Will you tell

me about the accomplishments of Duke Huan of Qi and Duke Wen of Jin?"

Mencius answered, "Confucius' disciples never talked about Duke Huan of Qi or Duke Wen of Jin, so their stories have not been passed down, and I have never heard about them either. If Your Highness insists my discussing something, I would like to talk about the kingly way of unifying the world with virtue."

King Xuan asked, "With what kind of virtue can the world be unified?"

Mencius said, "No man can be prevented from unifying the world if he unifies it by making the lives of the people stable."

……

Mencius said, "One really means it when he tells another: 'I cannot hold Mount Tai under my arms and carry it across the North Sea.' But when he tells another: 'I am unable to break a branch from a tree for an old man,' what he really means is he will not do it, not that he is unable to do it. Your not practicing a policy of benevolence is different from not holding Mount Tai under your arms and crossing the North Sea, but is the same as not breaking a branch for an old man. It does not mean that you are not able to do it, but that you will not do it."

Extend your respect for your aged parents to all the aged, and extend your love for your own children to all children. If one rules his kingdom with this principle in mind, then to unify the world will be as easy as turning his palms over. The *Book of Songs* says, 'Treat one's wife according to the rites, and extend the rites to brothers and then to the administration of one's family and country.' This means it is right to extend one's benevolent heart to other things. So Your Highness can keep the world stable if you extend your favor from the near to the distant. Otherwise, you would not be able to keep your own wife and children.

齐宣王问孟子："您可以给我讲讲齐桓公、晋文公称霸诸侯的事吗？"

孟子回答说："孔子的学生们没有谈到过齐桓公、晋文公的事，所以没有传下来，我也不曾听说过。您如果一定让我说，我就说说用道德的力量统一天下的'王道'吧！"

齐宣王问："要有什么样的道德才能统一天

下呢?"

孟子说:"如果为着百姓们的生活安定而去统一天下,是没有人能够阻挡得了的。"

……

孟子说:"如果对人说挟起泰山跨越北海的事我做不到,这是真的做不到。但如果对人说为老人折取树技的事我做不到,这是不肯去做,而不是做不到。王的不行仁政不是属于挟泰山跨北海一类,而是属于为老人折枝一类的。就是说不是做不到,而是不肯去做。由尊敬自己的老人,从而推广到尊敬所有的老人;爱护自己的儿女,从而推广到爱护所有人家的儿女。如果治理国家能从这一原则出发,统一天下则易如翻掌。《诗经》上说:'依礼对待妻子,再推广到兄弟,进而治理一家一国。'这就是把仁爱之心扩大到其它方面就可以了。所以说把您的恩惠由近及远地推广开去,就可以安定天下。否则,只怕连自己的妻子儿女都保不住。"

二、梁惠王下篇
King Hui of Liang, Part Two

《孟子》之第二篇。主要记孟子和齐宣王关于好乐、狩猎、和邻国交往、毁明堂以及伐燕事的问答。本篇共 16 章，节选其中 11 章。

孟子一行来到齐国稷下学宫的第二天，齐宣王率领文武百官在王宫东门外举行了隆重的欢迎仪式，旌旗猎猎，礼炮轰鸣，场面热烈肃穆。齐宣王封孟子为卿，孟子给齐宣王讲"保民而王，莫之能御也"的道理。

2.3 齐宣王问曰："交邻国有道乎？"孟子对曰："有。惟仁者为能以大事小，是故汤事葛，文王事昆夷。惟智者为能以小事大，故太王事獯鬻，勾践事吴。以大事小者，乐天者也；以小事大者，畏天者也。乐天者保天下，畏天者保其国。"

《梁惠王下篇·3》节选

汤事葛：汤，商王朝的建立者，亦称成汤。葛，古国名，嬴姓，故城在今河南省宁陵县北十五里，后为汤所灭。汤灭葛之前商汤曾服事葛伯。**文王事昆夷**：文王，周王朝的建立者，即周文王。昆夷亦作混夷，周初的西戎国名。文王事昆夷的详情已不可考。**太王事獯鬻**：太王亦作大王，即古公亶父，古代周族领袖，周文王祖父。獯鬻亦作薰育。当时北方少数民族。**勾践事吴**：越王勾践被吴王夫差打败，逃到会稽山，卑辞厚礼向吴国求和，自己为吴王当马前卒。后终于报仇，灭了吴国。

King Xuan of Qi asked Mencius, "Are there any principles that must be followed in dealing with neighboring kingdoms?"

Mencius said, "Yes. A benevolent person would serve the weak even though he is strong. So Tang of Shang served Count Ge and King Wen served Kun Yi. A wise man would serve the strong if he is weak. So King Tai served Xun Yu and Gou Jian served Fu Chai. The strong who serves the weak can adapt himself to all circumstances; the weak who serves the strong is cautious in everything. The one who can adapt to all circumstances can keep the world at peace and the one who is cautious in everything can keep his kingdom safe."

Notes: Tang served Count Ge: Tang was the founder of the Shang Dynasty, also called Cheng Tang. Ge was an ancient kingdom. The surname of its king was Ying. The capital city of Ge was 15 *li* north of present day Ningling County, Henan Province. Ge was later destroyed by Tang, but Tang had served Count Ge previously.

King Wen served Kun Yi: King Wen was the founder of the Zhou Dynasty. Kun Yi was also called Hun Yi, which was the name of a kingdom of the Western Rong tribe. There is no detailed record of this event.

King Tai served Xun Yu: King Tai was also called King Da, and his name was Gu Gong Tan Fu. He was the grandfather of King Wen and the leader of the Zhou nationality in ancient times. Xun Yu was the name of a northern tribe.

Gou Jian served Fu Chai: Gou Jian, king of Yue, was defeated by Fu Chai, king of Wu. He fled to Mount Kuaiji and sued for peace with humble words and generous gifts. He himself served as a groom to the king of Wu. Later he destroyed Wu.

齐宣王问孟子:"和邻国交往有什么必须遵循的原则吗?"

孟子回答说:"有的。仁德的人可以以大事小,所以商汤曾服事葛伯,文王曾服事昆夷。聪明的人可以以小事大,所以太王曾服事獯鬻,勾践曾服事夫差。以大事小的人能够随遇而安;以小事大的人谨小慎微。随遇而安的人可以安定天下,谨小慎微的人可以保全自己的国家。"

2.4 齐宣王见孟子于雪宫。王曰:"贤者亦有此乐乎?"孟子对曰:"有。人不得,则非其上矣。不得而非其上者,非也;为民上而不与民同乐者,亦非也。乐民之乐者,民亦乐其乐;忧民之忧者,民亦忧其忧。乐以天下,忧以天下,然而不王者,未之有也。"

《梁惠王下篇·4》节选

King Xuan of Qi received Mencius at Snow Palace. The king asked, "Do virtuous man too have such enjoyment as this?"

Mencius answered, "Yes. They would blame the kings if they did not have such enjoyments. It is wrong to do so, but it is also wrong for a king not to share his enjoyments with his people. If a king takes his people's delights as his own delights, then his people will take his delights as their own; if a king takes his people's sorrows as his own sorrows, then his people will take his sorrows as their own. Any king who shares delights and sorrows with his people is sure to dominate the world."

齐宣王在他的离宫雪宫里会见孟子,宣王问:"有才德的人也有这种游乐吗?"

孟子答道:"有的。如果他们得不到这种游乐,就会埋怨国君了。虽然因为得不到这种游乐就埋怨国君,是不对的。但作为一国之君有快乐而不能与他的百姓同享，也是不对的。如果国君以百姓的欢乐为自己的欢乐，百姓也会以国君的欢乐为自己的欢乐；国君以百姓的忧愁为自己的忧愁，百姓也会以国君的忧愁为自己的忧愁。和天下百姓同忧同乐的国君，就能使天下归服于他。"

2.5 齐宣王问曰："人皆谓我毁明堂，毁诸？已乎？"孟子对曰："夫明堂者，王者之堂也。王欲行王政，则勿毁之矣。"

《梁惠王下篇·5》节选

明堂：古代帝王宣明政教的地方。凡朝会、祭祀、庆赏、选士、养老、教学等大典，均在此进行。

King Xuan of Qi asked Mencius, "Many people have advised me to pull down the Great Hall. What is your opinion?"

Mencius answered, "The Great Hall is the place where a virtuous king practices a policy of benevolence to dominate the world. Do not pull it down if Your Highness wishes to practice a policy of benevolence."

齐宣王问孟子:"别人都劝我拆毁明堂,您说是拆还是不拆好?"

孟子答道:"明堂是有德政而又能统一天下的君主施王政的地方。您如果想实行王政,就不要拆毁它。"

2.6 孟子谓齐宣王曰:"王之臣有托其妻子于其友而之楚游者,比其反也,则冻馁其妻子,则如之何?"王曰:"弃之。"曰:"士师不能治士,则如之何?"王曰:"已之。"曰:"四境之内不治,则如之何?"王顾左右而言他。

《梁惠王下篇·6》

Mencius asked King Xuan of Qi, "If one of your officials were to ask a friend to look after his wife and children while he himself went on official business to Chu, but when he returned found his wife and children suffering from hunger and cold, what should he do to such a friend?"

The king said, "Break off all relation with him."

Mencius said, "What should be done if a commander cannot keep his officers under control?"

The king said, "He should be dismissed from his post."

Mencius said, "What if a kingdom is not well governed?"

The king glanced nervously to left and right, and changed the subject.

孟子对齐宣王说:"您有一个臣子把妻子儿女托给一个朋友照顾,自己到楚国去了。等他从楚国回来,他的妻子儿女正在挨饿受冻。对待这样的朋友,应该怎么办?"

宣王说:"和他绝交。"

孟子说:"假如掌刑罚的官员不能管好他的下级,那该怎么办?"

宣王说:"撤掉他。"

孟子说:"假如国家没有治理好,那又该怎么办?"

宣王回过头来左右看看,把话题扯到别处去了。

2.7 孟子见齐宣王,曰:"所谓故国者,非谓有乔木之谓也,有世臣之谓也。王无亲臣矣,昔者所进,今日不知其亡也。"王曰:"吾何以识其不才而舍之?"曰:"国君进贤,如不得已,将使卑逾尊,疏逾戚,可不慎与?左右皆曰贤,未可也;诸大夫皆曰贤,未可也;国人皆曰贤,然后察之;见贤焉,然后用之。左右皆曰不可,勿听;诸大夫皆曰不可,勿听;国人皆曰不可,然后察之;见不可焉,然后去之。左右皆曰可杀,勿听;诸大夫皆曰可杀,勿听;国人皆曰可杀,然后察之;见可杀焉,然后杀之。故曰,国人杀之也。如此,然后可以为民父母。"

Mencius had an audience with King Xuan of Qi and said to him: "When we call a country ancient it is not because it has ancient and tall trees, but because it has venerable and respected officials. Now Your Highness does not trust worthy officials; the capable ones selected in the past have all gone."

King Xuan of Qi asked, "How do I know who is incompetent so that I can dismiss him?"

Mencius answered, "When a ruler promotes worthy men to be officials, if there are none immediately suitable he may have to promote the lowly above the noble and the distant above the intimate. Does he therefore not have to be very careful in his selection? But how does one distinguish the good from the bad? You should not believe him if your aide says a certain person is competent; nor should you believe him if a senior official says so. But when all the people in your kingdom say so, you should find out if he really is competent, and employ him only after that. You should not believe him if your aide says a certain person is incompetent, nor should you believe him if a senior official says so. But when all the people in your kingdom say so, you should find out if he really is incompetent, and dismiss him only after that. You should not believe him if your aide says a certain person should be executed, nor should you believe him if a senior official says so. But when all the people in your kingdom say so, you should find out if he really should be executed, and execute him only after that. That means that it was really the people who executed him. Only in this way can a king be the father and mother of his people."

　　孟子谒见齐宣王，对他说道："我们平时所说的古国，不是说那个国家里有古老高大的树木，而是指有功高德望的老臣。您现在没有亲信的大臣，过去选用的有才能的人今天都不在位了。"
　　宣王问："怎样去识别那些无才能的人而不用他呢？"
　　孟子答道："国君选拔人才，如迫不得已要用新人，就是要把卑贱者提拔到尊贵者之上，把疏远者提拔到亲近者之上，对这样的选拔能够不慎重吗？怎样识别人好坏呢？如果您亲近的大臣们说某人好，您不可轻信。大夫们也说他好，也不可轻信。全国的人都说他好，您就要去了解,如果发现他真有才干,然后再任用他。如果您亲近的大臣们说某人坏,您不要轻信。大夫们也说他坏,也不要轻信。全国人都说他坏,您就要去了解,如果发现他真的很坏,就罢免他。如果您亲近的大臣们都说某人可杀,您不要轻信。大夫们也说这人可杀,您也不要轻信。全国的人都说他该杀,您就去了解,如果发现他真应该杀掉,再杀掉他。所以说,这是秉承全国人民的意志杀掉他的。这样的国君,才可以做百姓的父母。"

2.8 齐宣王问曰:"汤放桀,武王伐纣,有诸?"孟子对曰:"于传有之。"曰:"臣弑其君,可乎?"曰:"贼仁者谓之'贼',贼义者谓之'残',残贼之人谓之'一夫'。闻诛一夫纣矣,未闻弑君也。"

《梁惠王下篇·8》

汤放桀:汤,殷商开国之君。据传夏朝最后的国王桀暴虐无道,汤兴兵讨伐,最后把他流放到南巢(在今安徽省巢县东北)。**武王伐纣**:商纣王残暴无道,周武王兴兵讨伐,纣王大败,自焚而死。

King Xuan of Qi asked Mencius, "Is it true that Tang of the Shang Dynasty exiled Jie of the Xia Dynasty and King Wu of Zhou sent a punitive expedition against King Zhou of the Yin Dynasty?"

Mencius said, "It is so recorded in the history books."

King Xuan said, "Is it right for an official to kill his king?"

Mencius said, "One who does harm to benevolence is called a bandit; one who does harm to justice is called a savage. Such persons are autocrats. I have heard that King Wu of Zhou killed an autocrat by the name of Zhou of the Shang Dynasty; I have never heard that he killed his king."

Notes: ① Tang exiled Jie: Tang, the founder of the Yin Shang Dynasty. It is said that Jie, the last king of the Xia Dynasty, was a tyrant. Tang overthrew him and exiled him to Nan Chao (now in the northeast of Chaoxian County, Anhui Province).

② King Wu sent a punitive expedition against Zhou: King Zhou of the Shang Dynasty was a tyrant. King Wu of the Zhou Dynasty revolted and defeated him in battle, whereupon the latter burned himself to death.

齐宣王问孟子："商汤流放夏桀，武王讨伐殷纣，有这样的事吗？"

孟子说："史籍上是有这样的记载。"

宣王说："作臣子的杀掉君主，这应该吗？"

孟子说："败坏仁政的人叫'贼'，破坏道义的人叫'残'，残贼之人叫做'独夫'。我只听说过周武王诛杀了独夫商纣，没有听说他是以臣弑君。"

2.9 孟子见齐宣王，曰："为巨室，则必使工师求大木。工师得大木，则王喜，以为能胜其任也。匠人斲而小之，则王怒，以为不胜其任矣。"

《梁惠王下篇·9》节选

工师：古代官名，为各种工匠的主管官。

Mencius had an audience with King Xuan of Qi and said, "In building a big palace, the master craftsman is sent to look for big timber. When he finds it, Your Highness is delighted and thinks the master craftsman competent. But when carpenters whittle it before using it, Your Highness is not delighted, and thinks them incompetent.

孟子谒见齐宣王,说:"建筑一座大的宫殿,必定派工师去寻找大树。工师找到了大树,王就很高兴,认为工师是称职的。木匠要使其成材料必须将其砍削,王就不高兴,认为木匠是不称职的。"

2.10 齐人伐燕,胜之。宣王问曰:"或谓寡人勿取,或谓寡人取之,以万乘之国伐万乘之国,五旬而举之,人力不至于此。不取,必有天殃。取之,何如?"孟子对曰:"取之而燕民悦,则取之。古之人有行之者,武王是也。取之而燕民不悦,则勿取。古之人有行之者,文王是也。以万乘之国伐万乘之国,箪食壶浆,以迎王师,岂有他哉?避水火也。如水益深,如火益热,亦运而已矣。"

《梁惠王下篇·10》

万乘之国:周制,王畿方千里,能出兵车万乘。战国时也指拥有万辆兵车的大国。战国晚世"万乘之国七"(刘向《战国策·序》)。**箪食壶浆**:箪(dān),古代盛饭的竹器。浆,古代称以米熬成的汁,古人用以代酒。

Qi attacked Yan and defeated it. King Xuan of Qi consulted Mencius: "Some people urge me not to annex Yan, while others advise me to seize the chance to annex it. I think it must be the will of Heaven, not human power, for a kingdom of ten thousand chariots to defeat another kingdom of the same strength in fifty days. Heaven will punish me if I go against its will and do not annex Yan. So, shall I annex it?"

Mencius answered, "Annex it if the people of Yan are delighted to be annexed. That was done in ancient times, for example, by King Wu of Zhou. Do not annex it if the people of Yan are not delighted to be annexed. There is again a precedent in ancient times, for example, in the case of King Wen of Zhou. Qi attacked Yan, which was of the same strength, but the people of Yan welcomed your army with wine and rice. This meant that they looked forward to liberation from the cruel rule of the king of Yan. But if the annexation brings more disasters to the people of Yan, it will be a change of form, not content."

齐国军队攻打燕国,大获全胜。齐宣王问孟子:"有人劝我不要吞并燕国,也有人劝我趁机吞并它。我想,一个万乘之国去攻打一个同样的大国,只用五十天就打了下来,光凭人力是不行的,恐怕这是天意吧。如果我现在不吞并燕国,这有违天意,上天会降罪的。所以,吞并它好吗?"

孟子答道:"吞并它,如果燕国的老百姓高兴,您就吞并它。古时候有人这样做过,周武王便是。如果燕国的老百姓不高兴,您就不要吞并它。古时候也有人这样做过,周文王便是。以齐国这样的大国去攻打同样强大的燕国,燕国的老百姓却送饭送酒欢迎您的军队,这没有别的意思,只不过他们盼望着早些脱离燕国统治者水深火热的统治罢了。如果齐国吞并燕国后,更加深了燕国百姓的灾难,那只不过是换汤不换药而已。"

2.11 （孟子）曰："今燕虐其民，王往而征之，民以为将拯己于水火之中也，箪食壶浆以迎王师。若杀其父兄，系累其子弟，毁其宗庙，迁其重器，如之何其可也？天下固畏齐之强也，今又倍地而不行仁政，是动天下之兵也。王速出令，反其旄倪，止其重器，谋于燕众，置君而后去之，则犹可及止也。"

《梁惠王下篇·11》节选

齐国吞并了燕国，其他诸侯国计划伐齐救燕。齐宣王问计于孟子，孟子作了以上回答。

Mencius said, "Your Highness mounted an expedition to punish the tyrannous king of Yan. The people there thought you would liberate them from disaster, and so they provided wine and rice to your army. But Your Highness killed their fathers and brothers, kidnapped their children, destroyed their ancestral temples and robbed them of their treasures. How could Your Highness do such things? All the other kingdoms fear the might of Qi now that it has annexed Yan and doubled the size of its territory. But you are even more tyrannical, and this causes the other kingdoms to arm against Qi. Your Highness should give orders immediately to repatriate all prisoners of war, stop looting, consult with the people of Yan to designate a new ruler for Yan and withdraw your army from there. In this way, it might not be too late to stop the other kingdoms from sending armies against you."

孟子对齐宣王说:"现在,燕国的君主虐待百姓,您去征伐他,那里的老百姓以为您能把他们从水深火热的苦难中解救出来,所以他们送饭送酒慰劳齐军。而您呢,却杀死他们的父兄,掳掠他们的子弟,毁坏他们的宗庙,掠走他们国家的宝器。这怎么能行呢? 天下各国本来就害怕齐国强大,现在齐国吞并了燕国,土地扩大了一倍,而且更加暴虐无道,这自然会招致各国要攻伐齐国。您应该赶快发布命令,遣回燕国俘虏,停止掠夺燕国的宝器,再和燕国有关人士商量,择立新燕王,然后从燕国撤军,这样做好像还来得及使各国停止对齐国兴兵问罪。"

2.12 孟子曰:"凶年饥岁,君之民老弱转乎沟壑,壮者散而之四方者,几千人矣;而君之仓廪实,府库充,有司莫以告,是上慢而残下也。曾子曰:'戒之戒之!出乎尔者,反乎尔者也。'夫民今而后得反之也。君无尤焉!君行仁政,斯民亲其上,死其长矣。"

《梁惠王下篇·12》节选

曾子:孔子弟子曾参。邹国和鲁国发生了冲突。邹穆公对孟子说:"在这次冲突中,我有三十三位官员牺牲了,而老百姓却没有死一个,我要杀他们,又杀不了这么多;不杀他们,他们眼看着长官被杀却不上前营救,实在可恨,您说该怎么办?"孟子作了以上回答。

Mencius answered, "In famine years the aged and the weak of your people starved to death, and the young and the strong, in their thousands, fled the disaster. Yet your granaries were filled with grains and your warehouses were full of treasures. But none of your officials reported the situation to you. This means that the exalted ones not only failed to succour the people, but made their plight worse. Zeng Zi said: 'Beware! Others will treat you in the same way as you treat them.' Now your people have got the opportunity to take their revenge. Your Highness should not blame them. If you practice a policy of benevolence, your people will naturally cherish their superiors and sacrifice their lives for them."

Notes: Zeng Zi: Zeng Shen, one of Confucius' disciples.

孟子对邹穆公说:"当荒年饥岁,您的百姓中年老体弱的饿死在荒野,年轻力壮的四处逃荒,这样的人不下一千吧,而您的谷仓中堆满了粮食,府库里堆满了财宝,对这种情形您的有关官员谁也不向您报告。这就是在上位的人不关心老百姓的疾苦,还要残害他们。曾子曾经说过:'要警惕呀!要警惕呀!你怎样对待别人,别人就怎样回报你。'现在,您的百姓得到报复的机会了。您不应该责备百姓,您如果实行仁政，您的百姓自然会爱护他们的上级，甘心情愿为他们的长官卖命了。"

2.13 滕文公问曰："滕，小国也，间于齐、楚。事齐乎？事楚乎？"孟子对曰："是谋非吾所能及也。无已，则有一焉：凿斯池也，筑斯城也，与民守之，效死而民弗去，则是可为也。"

《梁惠王下篇·13》

滕文公：滕国国君。孟子的主张是：为国当自立，不做大国的附庸。

Duke Wen of Teng asked Mencius, "Teng is a weak kingdom lying between two big kingdoms, Qi and Chu. Should I serve Qi or Chu?"

Mencius answered, "This is not a question which I am qualified to answer. If Your Highness insists on my preferring advice, I have only one suggestion: Your Highness should deepen the city moat and consolidate the city walls, and defend your kingdom together with the people. Your kingdom may survive if the people stand firm and are willing to sacrifice their lives to defend it."

Note:Duke Wen of Teng:King of Teng . The essence of Mencius' suggestion is that Teng continue as an independent kingdom rather than become subservient to any big kingdom.

滕文公问孟子:"滕国是一个弱小的国家,处在齐国和楚国两个大国中间,我们是依附齐国呢,还是依附楚国呢?"

孟子回答说:"这个问题不是我能够决定的,如果您一定要我说,那我就只有一个主意:把护城河挖深,把城墙加固,和老百姓一道来保卫它,如果老百姓肯用生命来保卫国家,那就有希望了。"

三、公孙丑上篇
Gongsun Chou, Part One

《孟子》之第三篇。孟子和弟子公孙丑论王霸之业。本篇共9章，对其9章内容有所节选。

公元前333年，东方六国在苏秦的组织和参与下，于洹水（今河南省境内）举行会盟，制定"合纵抗秦"的政策。齐威王以东方大国的身分坐了第二把交椅。齐威王很是得意，雄心勃勃要恢复齐恒公的霸主地位。孟子却对他说："五霸者，三王之罪人也！"大臣们一个个要杀孟子。

3.1 公孙丑问曰:"夫子当路于齐,管仲、晏子之功,可复许乎?"孟子曰:"子诚齐人也,知管仲、晏子而已矣。或问乎曾西曰:'吾子与子路孰贤?'曾西蹴然曰:'吾先子之所畏也。'曰:'然则吾子与管仲孰贤?'曾西艴然不悦,曰:'尔何曾比予于管仲?管仲得君如彼其专也,行乎国政如彼其久也,功烈如彼其卑也;尔何曾比予于是?'"曰:"管仲,曾西之所不为也,而子为我愿之乎?"

《公孙丑上篇·1》节选

公孙丑:孟子弟子。**管仲、晏子**:管仲,齐桓公之相;晏子,即晏婴,齐景公之相。**曾西**:鲁人,曾参之子。**子路**:孔子弟子,即仲由。

Gongsun Chou asked, "If you were in power in

Qi, could you achieve what Guan Zhong and Yan Zi had achieved?"

Mencius said, "You really are a native of Qi! You know only Guan Zhong and Yan Zi. Someone once asked Zeng Xi: 'Who is more virtuous, you or Zilu?' Zeng Xi said uneasily: 'How dare I compare myself with Zilu, who is esteemed highly by my father?' That man asked again, 'Who is more virtuous, you or Guan Zhong?' Zeng Xi answered unhappily: 'Why compare me with Guan Zhong? His achievements were not great enough, though he enjoyed the perfect trust of Duke Huan of Qi and was in power for a long time. Why should you contrast me with him?'" Mencius continued, "While Zeng Xi would not compare himself with Guan Zhong, do you think I will do that?"

Notes: Gongsun Chou: A disciple of Mencius.

Guan Zhong, Yan Zi: Guan Zhong, prime minister of Duke Huan of Qi; Yan Zi, also named Yan Ying, prime minister of Duke Jing of Qi.

Zeng Xi: Son of Zeng Zi, from the State of Lu.

Zilu: A disciple of Confucius, also named Zhong You.

公孙丑问:"您如果在齐国当政,能够建立像管仲、晏子一样的功业吗?"

孟子说:"你真是一个齐国人,只晓得管仲、晏子。曾经有人问曾西:'你和子路相比,谁更强一些?'曾西不安地说:'他是我父亲所敬重的人,我怎敢和他相比?'那人又问曾西:'那你和管仲相比,谁更强一些?'曾西马上不高兴地说:'你为什么拿我和管仲比?管仲得到了齐桓公完全的信赖,执掌国家政权的时间那么长久,而功绩却不大。你为什么拿我和他相比呢?'"停了一会儿,孟子又说:"曾西都不愿和管仲相提并论,你以为我会学他吗?"

3.2 (孟子)曰:"我知言,我善养吾浩然之气。""敢问何谓浩然之气?"曰:"难言也。其为气也,至大至刚,以直养而无害,则塞于天地之间。其为气也,配义与道;无是,馁也。是集义所生者,非义袭而取之也。行有不慊于心,则馁矣。我故曰,告子未尝知义,以其外之也。必有事焉,而勿正,心勿忘，勿助长也。"

《公孙丑上篇·2》节选

浩然之气：孟子是指一种最高尚的道德境界。朱熹称之为"天地之正气"。

Mencius said, "I am good at analyzing the words of others, but I am also good at cultivating the great moral force."

Gongsun Chou asked again: "What is the great moral force?"

Mencius said, "It is difficult to explain it clearly in a few words. Such a force is both wide and strong. If it is cultivated with justice and not harmed in any way, it will exist all over the universe. Such a force must be in harmony with justice and the natural way, otherwise it will not be powerful. Such a force is generated after long accumulation of justice and cannot be attained overnight. If an unjust act is done, that force will be gone. That is why I said Gao Zi did not understand justice, he took justice as something outside his thought. We should take care to cultivate it, but we should not cultivate it for any particular purpose. We should constantly keep that in mind, but we should not do it in haste.

孟子说:"我善于分析别人的言辞,也善于培养我的浩然之气。"

公孙丑又问:"什么叫做浩然之气呢?"

孟子说:"这很难一下子讲清楚。这种气至大至刚。用正义去培养它,不能稍有伤害,这种气就会存在于天地之间,无所不在。这种气还必须和义与道相配合,否则就没有什么力量了。这种气是由正义的长期积累所产生的,不是一朝一夕所能取得的。只要做一件于心有愧的事,这种气就空了。所以我说,告子不懂得义,他把义看做心外之物。我们一定要注意培养它,但不一定有什么特定的目的。时时刻刻记住它,但也不可操之过急。"

3.3　孟子曰:"以力假仁者霸,霸必有大国;以德行仁者王,王不待大——汤以七十里,文王以百里。以力服人者,非心服也,力不赡也;以德服人者,中心悦而诚服也，如七十子之服孔子也。"

《公孙丑上篇·3》节选

七十子：孔门弟子中身通六艺者的通称。

Mencius said, "The state that forces other lords to submit in the name of benevolence and justice will have to be a strong and powerful one. The state that unifies the world with policy of benevolence and justice need not be a strong and powerful one. King Tang of the Shang Dynasty and King Wen of the Zhou Dynasty unified the world starting with only 70 square li and 100 square li of land, respectively. When one dominates others by force, they do not submit to him sincerely, but do so because they are not powerful enough to resist. When one dominates others by morality, they submit gladly, as his 70 disciples respected Confucius."

孟子说："依靠实力假借仁义称霸诸侯的，一定是强大的国家。依靠道德来实行仁义统一天下的不一定是强大的国家——汤就仅以七十里国土，文王也仅以百里国土就统一了天下。以力服人者，人不会心服，只是因为人家没有对抗的实力；以道德服人者，人才会心悦诚服，好像孔子的七十多位弟子归服他那样。"

3.4 孟子曰："仁则荣，不仁则辱；今恶辱而居不仁，是犹恶湿而居下也。如恶之，莫如贵德而尊士，贤者在位，能者在职；国家闲暇，及是时，明其政刑。虽大国，必畏之矣。

"今国家闲暇，及是时，般乐怠敖，是自求祸也。祸福无不自己求之者。诗云：'永言配命，自求多福。'太甲曰：'天作孽，犹可违；自作孽，不可活。'此之谓也。"

《公孙丑上篇·4》节选

Mencius said, "Practicing a policy of benevolence leads to glory; otherwise humiliation occurs. Nowadays, men in power, although they detest humiliation, they do not practice a policy of benevolence. This is like detesting moisture but living in low-lying land. If they really detest humiliation, they should attach great importance to morality and respect scholars, employ virtuous persons as officials and assign capable persons to important posts. If they took advantage of the time when there is no domestic trouble or foreign invasion to put their governments to rights, then even strong and powerful neighbors would have cause to fear them. Now is a time of peace, but the men in power seek luxuries and pleasures, ignoring government affairs. This is tantamount to seeking calamities. Both fortunes and misfortunes are invited by oneself. The *Book of Songs* says also:'The Zhou Dynasty should accomplish the mandate of Heaven and seek more fortunes. ' The *Book of History* says,'When Heaven sends down calamities, there is hope of weathering them; when man brings them down upon himself, there is no hope of escape. ' "

孟子说:"如果实行仁政,就会得到荣耀;如果不行仁政,就会遭受屈辱。如今的执政者,都不想遭受屈辱但又不肯行仁政,这好比厌恶潮湿却又自居于低洼之地一样。假若真厌恶屈辱，就应该重道德而尊敬士人，使有德行的人居于相当的官位，有才能的人担任一定职务。国家无内忧外患，及时修明政治法典，纵使强大的邻国也会有所畏惧。

"如今国家没有内忧外患，执政者却追求享乐，尽情游玩，不理政事，这等于自寻其祸。祸与福都是自找的。《诗经》上说：'我们周朝的命运与天命相配，自己去寻找更多的幸福。'《尚书》中也说：'天灾尚可躲避，自作的罪孽，是逃不过惩罚的。'就是这个意思了。"

3.5 孟子曰："尊贤使能，俊杰在位，则天下之士皆悦，而愿立于其朝矣。"

《公孙丑上篇·5》节选

Mencius said, "A king should respect virtuous persons, employ capable persons and put outstanding persons in posts so as to give full play to their wisdom and capabilities. Then all the scholars in the world would be delighted and would like to serve in his kingdom."

孟子说:"尊重有道德的人,重用有才能的人,使杰出的人物都有发挥才干的机会。那么,天下的士子都会高兴,都愿意到这个国家供职。"

3.6　孟子曰:"人皆有不忍人之心。先王有不忍人之心,斯有不忍人之政矣。以不忍人之心,行不忍人之政,治天下可运之掌上。

"无恻隐之心,非人也;无羞恶之心,非人也;无辞让之心,非人也;无是非之心,非人也。恻隐之心,仁之端也;羞恶之心,义之端也;辞让之心,礼之端也;是非之心,智之端也。人之有是四端也,犹其有四体也。有是四端而自谓不能者,自贼者也;谓其君不能者,贼其君者也。凡有四端于我者,知皆扩而充之矣,若火之始然,泉之始达。苟能充之,足以保四海；苟不充之，不足以事父母。"

《公孙丑上篇·6》节选

Mencius said, "Everyone has a heart of mercy. Ancient emperors had hearts of mercy, so they practiced policies of mercy. It is as easy as turning the hand over to practice a policy of mercy with a heart of mercy. We can say a man is not a human being if he has no sense of sympathy; neither would he be a human being if he had no sense of shame, modesty, and right and wrong. A sense of sympathy is the beginning of being benevolent; a sense of shame is the beginning of being just; a sense of modesty is the beginning of being polite; and a sense of right and wrong is the beginning of being wise. Men are born with these four senses, as with their four limbs. One who possesses these four senses but still thinks himself incapable is giving himself up. And one who thinks his king incapable when his king possesses these four senses is giving his king up. If anyone who possesses these four senses can develop and cultivate them in a timely fashion, he will be like a spark spreading far and wide eventually or like a spring becoming a river eventually. He who develops and cultivates these senses in a timely fashion can protect the world. But he who cannot will not be able to support even his own parents."

孟子说:"每个人都有怜悯别人之心。先王因为有怜悯别人之心,则有怜悯别人的政治。以怜悯别人之心实施怜悯别人的政治,治理天下则易如翻掌。

"一个人如果没有同情心,简直就不是人了。如果没有羞耻之心、谦让之心、是非之心,也就不配为人了。同情之心是仁的萌芽,羞耻之心是义的萌芽,谦让之心是礼的萌芽,是非之心是智的萌芽。人有这四种心和有四肢一样是与生俱来的。具有这四种心的却认为自己不行的人是自暴自弃,认为其君主不行的人就是暴弃其君主。所以凡是具有这四种心的人,如果知道及早培养充实,发扬光大,就会像刚燃起的星星之火,终必可以燎原;刚流出的泉水,终必会汇成江河一样,便足以安定天下。假如不及早培养充实,发扬光大,便连父母也不知道赡养了。"

3.7 孟子曰："矢人岂不仁于函人哉？矢人唯恐不伤人，函人唯恐伤人。巫匠亦然。故术不可不慎也。孔子曰：'里仁为美。择不处仁，焉得智？'夫仁，天之尊爵也，人之安宅也。莫之御而不仁，是不智也。不仁、不智，无礼、无义，人役也。人役而耻为役，由弓人而耻为弓，矢人而耻为矢也。如耻之，莫如为仁。仁者如射：射者正己而后发；发而不中，不怨胜己者，反求诸己而已矣。"

《公孙丑上篇·7》

矢人：造箭之人。函人：造甲之人。巫：古代称能以舞降神的人。古人治病亦用巫，称巫医。匠：木工。

Mencius said, "Can arrow-makers be crueller than armorers? Arrow-makers fear that their arrows may not be able to hurt others; and armorers are afraid that their armor may not be able to withstand arrows. Sorcerers and carpenters are the same. Sorcerers fear their patients may not recover, and carpenters are afraid the patients may recover, and so the demand for coffins will slump. So, one should be very careful in choosing his profession. Confucius said, 'How can one become wise if one chooses to live where benevolence is absent?' Benevolence is the noblest quality in the world, and where it is is where men should dwell. It is not wise not to be benevolent when no one prevents you from being so. If a man is neither benevolent nor wise nor polite nor just, he can only serve as a slave to others. If a man feels ashamed of being a slave while he can only be a slave, it is like a bow-maker feeling ashamed of making bows or arrow-makers feeling ashamed of making arrows. If they are really ashamed of being what they are, they should practice benevolence. A benevolent man should be like an archer who takes part in a shooting match and adjusts his posture before shooting. If he misses the target, he should not blame the winners, but seek the cause in himself."

孟子说:"难道造箭的人比造甲的人更残忍

吗？造箭的人生怕他造的箭不能伤人，而造甲的人生怕他造的甲不能抵御利箭。做巫医的和木匠也是这样。巫医唯恐病人不得痊愈，而木匠唯恐病人好了，棺材卖不出去。所以选择职业不可不慎重。孔子说：'选择住处，如果不以仁者为邻，怎么能算明智呢？'仁是天地间最尊贵的，也是人最可靠的归宿。没有人来阻挡你，你却不仁，这是不明智的。不仁、不智，无礼、无义，这种人只能做别人的奴仆。做奴仆又自以为耻，就好比造弓的人以造弓为耻，造箭的人以造箭为耻一样。如果真以为耻，就不如好好地去行仁。有仁德的人好比参加射箭比赛的射手一样：先端正自己的姿势而后放箭，如果没有射中，也不要埋怨那些胜过自己的人，只在自己身上找原因就是了。"

3.8 孟子曰："子路，人告之以有过，则喜。禹闻善言，则拜。大舜有大焉，善与人同，舍己从人，乐取于人以为善。自耕稼、陶、渔以至为帝，无非取于人者。取诸人以为善，是与人为善者也。

故君子莫大乎与人为善。"

《公孙丑上篇·8》

禹：中国古代传说中的帝王，夏朝的开国君主。舜：中国古代传说中的帝王。

Mencius said, "Zilu was glad to have his errors pointed out, and Yu bowed down when he heard anything good. Shun was even more extraordinary. He was good at associating with others and learning their good points to remedy his own shortcomings. He had been a peasant, potter and fisherman before he became an emperor. He never ceased learning from others. Learning good points from others is doing good things together with others. The best virtue of a gentleman is to do good things together with others."

Notes: Yu: Legendary founder of the Xia Dynasty.
Shun: Legendary sage king.

孟子说："子路能够闻过则喜，大禹听到有益的言论便拜谢。舜帝更了不起，他善于和人交往，善于吸收别人的长处来克服自己的短处。

从他种庄稼、做瓦器、做渔夫一直到做帝王，没有停止过向别人学习。吸取别人的长处行善，就是和别人一同行善。所以君子最高的德行就是与人为善。"

3.9 孟子曰："伯夷，非其君，不事；非其友，不友。不立于恶人之朝，不与恶人言；立于恶人之朝，与恶人言，如以朝衣朝冠坐于涂炭。"

《公孙丑上篇·9》节选

Mencius said, "Boyi's principle of life was that he would not serve an unideal king, nor would he befriend an unideal friend, nor would he be an official in a court where evil persons were in power, nor would he talk with an evil person. He thought that to be an official in a court where evil persons were in power and to talk with evil persons was like sitting in a dirty place in court attire."

孟子说："伯夷这个人的处世原则是：不是他理想的君主，不去侍奉；不是他理想的朋友，不去结交。不仕于坏人当政之朝，不同坏人说话。他认为在坏人当政的国家做官，和坏人讲话，就好像穿戴着礼服礼帽坐在肮脏龌龊的地方会沾染自己。"

四、公孙丑下篇
Gongsun Chou, Part Two

《孟子》之第四篇。孟子提出"天时不如地利,地利不如人和","得道者多助,失道者寡助"的观点。本篇共14章,节选其中5章。

孟子对齐宣王说:"天时不如地利,地利不如人和。"又说,"得道者多助,失道者寡助。寡助之至,亲戚畔之;多助之至,天下顺之。"(《孟子·公孙丑下》)

4.1 孟子曰："天时不如地利，地利不如人和。三里之城，七里之郭，环而攻之而不胜。夫环而攻之，必有得天时者矣；然而不胜者，是天时不如地利也。城非不高也，池非不深也，兵革非不坚利也，米粟非不多也；委而去之，是地利不如人和也。故曰：域民不以封疆之界，固国不以山谿之险，威天下不以兵革之利。得道者多助，失道者寡助。寡助之至，亲戚畔之；多助之至，天下顺之。以天下之所顺，攻亲戚之所畔；故君子有不战，战必胜矣。"

《公孙丑下篇·1》

天时、地利、人和：天时、地利、人和是当时成语，而其内容时有所变。孟子在这里讲的天时是指阴睛寒暑之是否与攻战有利。地利则指高城深池、山川险阻。人和则指人心所向。三里之城，七里之郭：言其城小，古制一般为三里之城，五里之郭。"七里之郭"恐有误。

Mencius said, "Favourable weather is less important than advantageous terrain, and advantageous terrain is less important than unity among the people. For example, the inner city of a small city is not larger than three square *li*, and its outer city is not larger than seven square *li*. But an enemy cannot conquer it even after a long siege. During such a long time there must be favourable weather, but the enemy cannot break into it because favourable weather is less important than advantageous terrain. When city walls are high, ditches deep, weapons superior and grain abundant, but the defenders abandon the city and flee under attack by the enemy, it is because advantageous terrain is less important than unity among the people. So, it is said that national border alone can not stop people from fleeing, precipitous terrain alone can not insure the security of the state, and force alone can not subjugate the world. Practicing a policy of benevolence wins support from the people; otherwise the support of the people will be lost. If one loses the support of the people, even one's relatives will

◎公孙丑下篇 *Gongsun Chou, Part Two*

turn against one; if one wins the support of the people, all the people in the world will come to pledge allegiance. When a gentleman who has the support of the people attacks one who is opposed by the masses and deserted by his followers, he may win without fighting, and is sure to win if he does fight."

Notes: Favorable weather, advantageous terrain and unity among the people: Their meanings vary at different times. Favorable weather here means weather favorable for fighting; advantageous terrain indicates high city walls, deep ditches, dangerous rivers and precipitous mountains. Unity among the people refers to the common aspirations of the people.

Inner city and outer city: Generally, the inner city was three square *li* and outer city, five square *li* in area.

孟子说:"天时不如地利,地利不如人和。譬如一座小城,内城不过三里,外城不过七里。敌人长时间围攻而不能攻破它。在这么长时间围攻中,一定会有顺乎天时的时候,但却不能攻破它,这就是天时不如地利的道理。又譬如,城高池深,武器精良,粮食充足,然而敌人一来便弃城逃跑,这就是占有地利不如得人和。

所以说，单靠疆界不足以约束人民，单靠山川的险阻不足以保护国家的安全，单靠武力不足以威震天下。行仁政就得人心，不行仁政便失人心。失人心的结果，连亲戚都会背叛他；得人心的结果，天下的人都会归顺他。以天下民心所向攻击众叛亲离的人，那么，君子或者不战，而战，则必然胜利。"

4.2 （孟子）曰："天下有达尊三：爵一，齿一，德一。朝廷莫如爵，乡党莫如齿，辅世长民莫如德。"

《公孙丑下篇·2》节选

It is generally accepted that there are three valuable things: title of nobility, age and morality. In court, there is nothing more valuable than title of nobility; in the neighborhood, there is nothing more valuable than age. But as to assisting kings to rule over the people, there is nothing more valuable than morality.

孟子说："大家公认尊贵者有三：爵位，年

龄,道德。在朝廷中论爵位高低;在乡里论年龄大小;至于辅助君主治理国家自然以道德为上。"

4.3 (孟子)曰:"无处而馈之,是货之也。焉有君子而可以货取乎?"

《公孙丑下篇·3》节选

Meincius said:"Offering money to me with no reason amounted to an attempt to bribe me. Can a gentleman accept a bribe?"

孟子说:"没有正当理由而送我钱财,这等于用钱财收买我。哪里有君子可以用钱财收买的呢?"

4.9 (孟子)曰:"且古之君子,过则改之;今之君子,过则顺之。古之君子,其过也,如日月之食,民皆见之;及其更也,民皆仰之。今之君子,岂徒顺之,又从为之辞。"

《公孙丑下篇·9》节选

Mencius said, "A benevolent ruler in ancient times would correct his mistakes. But a ruler now would leave the mistake uncorrected and muddle through. The mistakes of ancient rulers were like solar and lunar eclipses—they were known to all people. After they corrected their mistakes, the people admired them all the more. But a ruler now would not only leave the mistakes uncorrected, he would make excuses for them."

孟子说:"古代有仁德的执政者,有错即改;今天的执政者,有了过错,竟将错就错。古代的执政者,他的过错像日蚀月蚀一般挂在天上,老百姓都看得见。当他们改正以后,老百姓更加敬仰他们。今天的执政者,不仅将错就错,还一定要编造一番假道理来为错误辩护。"

4.13 孟子去齐,充虞路问曰:"夫子若有不豫色然。前日虞闻诸夫子曰：'君子不怨天，不尤人。'"曰："彼一时，此一时也。五百年必有王者兴，其间必有名世者。由周而来，七百有余岁矣。以其数，则过矣；以其时考之，则可矣。夫天未欲平治天下也；如欲平治天下，当今之世，舍我其谁也？吾何为不豫哉？"

《公孙丑下篇·13》

Mencius left Qi. Chong Yu said to him on the way: "Sir, you look unhappy. I have heard you say, 'A gentleman should not blame neither Heaven nor man.'"

Mencius said, "That was then; now is now. History shows that one sage sovereign will rise every five hundred years, and there will also be a well-known person to assist him. It has now been seven hundred years since the Zhou Dynasty was founded, and it is time for another sage sovereign to come into the world. It might not be the will of God to keep the world at peace. But if it is, who else except I can do it? Why should I be unhappy?"

　　孟子离开齐国，在路上充虞问道："您的样子好像很不高兴。我从前听您说过：'君子不怨天尤人。'现在为什么这样呢？"

　　孟子说："彼一时，此一时也。时势不同，情况也随之改变。从历史来看，每过五百年就一定会有圣君兴起，也一定会有闻名于世的人才出世辅佐圣君。从周武王以来，到现在已经七百年了。计年数，已超过了五百年。论时势，现在正该圣君贤臣出世平定天下的时候。这是上天不愿使天下太平吧，如果要使天下太平，在当今之世，除了我，还有谁呢？我为什么不高兴呢？"

五、滕文公上篇
Duke Wen of Teng, Part One

《孟子》之第五篇。皆与滕文公论政,从滕定公死,滕文公为世子时即问丧礼于孟子,至滕文公执政"问为国"。本篇共5章,节选其中4章。

滕国世子(即后来的滕文公)和他的老师然友出使楚国,路过宋都彭城,一起拜访孟子,向孟子请教:如何为官,如何治国,如何服民,如何和大国交往等问题。孟子言必称尧舜,和他讲了人性本善的道理。

5.1 滕文公为世子，将之楚，过宋而见孟子。孟子道性善，言必称尧舜。

《滕文公上篇·1》节选

Duke Wen of Teng went to Chu when he was crown prince. On his way, he saw Mencius in Song. Mencius always mentioned Yao and Shun when he explained his theory that men are born good.

滕文公作太子的时候，有一次到楚国去，经过宋国时，会见了孟子。孟子言必称尧舜，和他讲了人性本善的道理。

5.2 （孟子）曰："上有好者，下必有甚焉者矣。君子之德，风也；小人之德，草也。草尚之风，必偃。"

《滕文公上篇·2》节选

Mencius said, "Inferiors are keen to do more of what their superiors are fond of doing. Gentlemen are like the wind and petty persons are like grass, which bends with the wind."

孟子说：" 在上位的人有什么爱好，下边的人一定爱得更加过分。君子好比风，小人好比草，风向哪边吹，草向哪边倒。"

5.3　孟子曰："民之为道也，有恒产者有恒心，无恒产者无恒心。苟无恒心，放辟邪侈，无不为已。及陷乎罪，然后从而刑之，是罔民也。焉有仁人在位罔民而可为也？是故贤君必恭俭礼下，取于民有制。"

《滕文公上篇·3》节选

Mencius said, "The basic situation is that the people observe moral concepts and codes of behavior only when they have regular incomes from their property. If they do not have regular incomes, they disregard morality. When a man does not have any kind of morality or code of behaviour, he will act wildly and in defiance of laws, and would do whatever he sees fit. It amounts to doing harm to him to punish him after he becomes a criminal. How can a humane ruler do such a thing? So a wise and able king must be conscientious in his administration, thrifty, treat his subordinates politely and, especially, should not levy taxes excessively."

孟子说:"人民的基本情况是,有固定产业收入的人才可能有一定的道德观念和行为准则,没有固定产业收入的人就不会有一定的道德观念和行为准则。假如一个人没有一定的道德观念和行为准则,他就会胡作非为违法乱纪,什么事都干得出来。等到他们犯了罪,再去处罚他们,这等于当政者害了他们。哪有仁德的执政者去干陷害人民的事呢?所以,贤明的君主一定要办事认真,节省用度,以礼待人,特别征收赋税要有限制。"

5.4　(孟子)曰:"且一人之身,而百工之所为备,如必自为而后用之，是率天下而路也。故曰，或劳心，或劳力；劳心者治人，劳力者治于人；治于人者食人，治人者食于人，天下之通义也。"

……

"尧以不得舜为己忧，舜以不得禹皋陶为己忧。夫以百亩之不易为己忧者，农夫也。分人以财谓之惠，教人以善谓之忠，为天下得人者谓之仁。是故以天下与人易，为天下得人难。孔子曰：'大哉尧之为君！惟天为大，惟尧则之，荡荡乎民无能名焉！君哉舜也！巍巍乎有天下而不与焉！'尧舜之治天下，岂无所用其心哉？亦不用于耕耳。"

《滕文公上篇·4》节选

皋陶（gāo yáo）：传为舜时之司法官。

Mencius said, "Then can a ruler do farming? Officials and ordinary people have their own tasks. Each person uses the products of many craftsmen. If everyone had to make everything he needed, life would come to a standstill. So, it is natural that some engage in mental work and some do manual work. Those who work with their brains rule, while those who labor are ruled. The ruled support others with their products, and the rulers are supported by others. This is a general principle."

"Yao was concerned that he might not be able to select such a talented person as Shun, and Shun was concerned that he might not be able to pick out such worthies as Yu and Gaoyao. It is for the farmers to worry about land being poorly cultivated. It is generous to distribute wealth to others; it is loyal to teach others the correct way to behave and it is benevolent to pick out talented people for the world. So it is easy to leave the kingdom to others, and it is difficult to select talents. So Confucius said, 'Yao was an extraordinary sovereign. Heaven's wisdom is limitless and only Yao could follow its ways. There were no words that ordinary people could find to praise his wisdom. Shun was an extraordinary sovereign also. Noble as sovereign, possessing the whole world, yet he labored himself all year long without seeking any private gain.' Did not Yao and Shun exert themselves to the utmost in ruling the state? But they did not engage in farming!"

孟子说:"那么,难道治理国家的人就能同时干得了各种工作吗?官吏有官吏的工作,百姓有百姓的工作。各种工匠制作的成品对每个人都是不可缺少的,如果每件东西都要自己制作出来才可以用,这是让执政者疲于奔命。所以我说,有的人从事脑力劳动,有的人从事体力劳动,脑力劳动者管理人,体力劳动者接受管理。被管理者用他的产品养活别人,管理者靠别人来养活,这是一个普遍的原则。"

……

孟子说:"尧以找不到舜这样的人才而忧虑,舜以找不到禹和皋陶这样的人才而忧虑。因自己的田地种不好而忧虑的,那是农夫。把钱财分给别人那叫惠,把正确的道理教给别人那叫忠,为天下太平而选拔贤人那是仁。把天下让给别人容易,而替天下选拔到杰出的人才就困难得多。所以孔子说:'尧是一位了不起的君主。天意是无限的，只有尧能够效法天。他的恩惠使老百姓不知如何称颂才好，舜也是一位了不起的君主，贵为天子，富有四海，整年为百姓辛劳而一点不谋私利。'尧舜之治天下，难道不用心思吗？只是不把心思用在种庄稼上罢了。"

六、滕文公下篇
Duck Wen of Teng, Part Two

《孟子》之第六篇。孟子提出"志士"、"勇士"和"大丈夫"的标准。本篇共10章,节选其中5章。

孟子对弟子们说:"从前齐景公田猎,用不合礼法的方法召唤猎场管理官员,该官员竟不予理会,齐景公准备将他治罪,可是他并不畏惧。孔子曾称赞过他'志士不忘在沟壑,勇士不忘丧其元。'孔子赞扬他什么呢?就赞扬他敢于依礼办事的精神。"(《孟子·滕文公下》)

6.1 孟子曰:"昔齐景公田,招虞人以旌,不至,将杀之。志士不忘在沟壑,勇士不忘丧其元。孔子奚取焉?取非其招不往也。"

《滕文公下篇·1》节选

旌(jīng):古代一种旗杆上用彩色羽毛做装饰的旗子。古代君王有所召唤,一定有相当的事物以见信。旌是召唤大夫用的,若召唤虞人,只能用皮冠。

Mencius said, "Once Duke Jing of Qi went hunting. He summoned the administrator of a piggery to confer honors on him, but the latter resisted his summons. Duke Jing wanted to have him executed, yet he was not scared. Confucius once praised him. A person with lofty ideals would not hesitate to have his corpse abandoned in the wilderness, and a courageous person would not spare his life to do what is right. What quality of the administrator of the piggery did Confucius appreciate? His spirit of doing everything according to the rites."

孟子说:"从前齐景公田猎,用不合礼法的

方法召唤猎场管理官员,该官员竟不予理会,齐景公准备将他治罪。可是他并不畏惧,孔子曾称赞过他。有志之士为坚守节操不怕弃尸荒野,勇敢的人见义而为不怕掉脑袋。孔子欣赏这位猎场管理官员什么呢?就欣赏他坚持依礼行事的精神。"

6.2 孟子曰:"是焉得为大丈夫乎?子未学礼乎?丈夫之冠也,父命之;女子之嫁也,母命之,往送之门,戒之曰:'往之女家,必敬必戒,无违夫子!'以顺为正者,妾妇之道也。居天下之广居,立天下之正位,行天下之大道;得志,与民由之;不得志,独行其道。富贵不能淫,贫贱不能移,威武不能屈,此之谓大丈夫。"

《滕文公下篇·2》节选

景春提出公孙衍、张仪"一怒而诸侯惧,安居而天下熄",应该称为大丈夫吗?孟子作了否定的回答。

Mencius said, "How could such persons be called gentlemen? Have you not studied the rites? When a boy reaches the age of twenty, a ceremony is held to celebrate his coming of age. His father gives him instruction. When a girl marries, her mother escorts her to the gate, cautioning her: 'At your new home, you must be filial and respectful to your father-in-law and mother-in-law, act cautiously and don't go against your husband's will.' The highest principle of female virtue is obedience. As for males, the guiding principle should be benevolence. His performance should conform to the rites and his behavior should be righteous and just. When he is in power, he should follow the right course together with the people; when he is not in power, he should stick to his own principles. Wealth and power cannot corrupt him, poverty can not sway his principles and threats cannot made him bend. Only such a person can be called a gentleman."

孟子说:"这怎么能称为大丈夫呢？你没学过礼吗？男子二十岁举行加冠礼时，父亲给以训导。女子出嫁的时候，母亲给以训导，送她到门口，告诫说:'到了婆家，一定要孝敬公婆，行为谨慎,听丈夫的话。'以顺从为最高原则,这是妇道。至于男子,应居之以仁,立之以礼,行之以义。得志时,和百姓一起走正道;不得志的时候,也能独自坚持正确的原则,富贵不乱其心,贫贱不变其志,威武不屈其节,这才是大丈夫。"

6.3 (孟子)曰:"丈夫生而愿为之有室,女子生而愿为之有家;父母之心,人皆有之。不待父母之命、媒妁之言,钻穴隙相窥,逾墙相从,则父母国人皆贱之。古之人未尝不欲仕也,又恶不由其道。不由其道而往者,与钻穴隙之类也。"

《滕文公下篇·3》节选

周霄问:"古代的君子主张做官吗?"孟子作了肯定的回答后又说作官要经正当途径。

Mencius said, "When a male child is born, his parents seek a wife for him. When a female child is born, her parents seek a husband for her. All parents are alike in this. But if children do not wait for the commands of their parents and the good offices of go-betweens, but make private arrangements by themselves, then not only their parents but all the people in the community will despise them. Of our forefathers none eschewed officialdom. But they hated to become officials without going through the proper procedure. To be an official without going through the proper procedure is like becoming engaged to be married privately: Everyone would look down upon such an official."

孟子说:"男孩子一生下来,父母便希望给他找到妻室;女孩子一生下来,父母便希望给她找到婆家。父母这样的心情,人人都有。但是,若不待父母之命,媒妁之言便私自来往相会,那么,父母以及社会上所有的人都会鄙视他。古人不是不想做官,而是讨厌不经正当途径而获得官位。不经正当途径而做官,正像男女私定终身一样为人瞧不起。"

6.5 (孟子)曰:"不行王政云尔;苟行王政,四海之内皆举首而望之，欲以为君；齐楚虽大，何畏焉？"

《滕文公下篇·5》节选

弟子万章问小国如果实行仁政，而周围大国不高兴怎么办？孟子讲了从前汤讨伐葛伯的经过后又说了上面的话。

I have nothing to say if the king of Song will not practice benevolent policies. But if he puts them into practice, all the people in the world are sure to look forward to his becoming their ruler. What is there to fear even though Qi and Chu are stronger?

孟子说："不实行仁政便罢了，如果真实行仁政，天下百姓莫不翘首盼望他来做新君王。齐国和楚国虽然强大，又有什么可怕的呢？"

6.6　孟子谓戴不胜曰："子欲子之王之善与？我明告子。有楚大夫于此，欲其子之齐语也，则使齐人傅诸？使楚人傅诸？"曰："使齐人傅之。"曰："一齐人傅之，众楚人咻之，虽日挞而求其齐也，不可得矣；引而置之庄岳之间数年，虽日挞而求其楚，亦不可得矣。子谓薛居州，善士也，使之居于王所。在于王所者，长幼卑尊皆薛居州也，王谁与为不善？在王所者，长幼卑尊皆非薛居州也，王谁与为善？一薛居州，独如宋王何？"

《滕文公下篇·6》

戴不胜：宋国大臣。庄岳：齐国都城临淄繁华街道名。薛居州：宋人。

Mencius said to Dai Busheng, "Do you wish your king to follow what is right? I will tell you how to do it. If there is an official from Chu who wishes his son to learn the Qi dialect, should he employ a Qi teacher or a Chu teacher to instruct him?"

Dai Busheng said, "Of course, a Qi teacher."

Mencius said, "If a Qi teacher is employed to instruct him to speak the Qi dialect, but there are many Chu people speaking the Chu dialect all a-round him, he will not be able to learn the Qi dialect even if he is forced to try every day. But if he were sent to live in the center of Linzi, the capital of Qi, for a few years, he would not be able to speak the Chu dialect even if he were forced to try every day. You have said that Xue Juzhou is a good man and if he is assigned to live in the palace to influence the king of Song, the king will follow what is right. Now, if all the people in the palace are good like Xue Juzhou, with whom would the king commit wrong? But if all the people in the palace are not good like Xue Juzhou, with whom would he do good? Do you think Xue Juzhou would be able to influence the king of Song single-handed?"

Notes: Dai Busheng: A high official of Song.
Xue Juzhou: A Song personage.

孟子对戴不胜说："你想要你们宋国的君王从善吗？我明白告诉你。这里有位楚国的官员，希望他的儿子学说齐国话，那么，是找齐国人来这里教他呢？还是找个楚国人来这里教他呢？"

戴不胜说："当然要找个齐国人来这里教他。"

孟子说："一个齐国人来教他说齐国话，却有许多楚国人在他周围说楚国话干扰他，纵使每天逼迫他说齐国话，也是不可能的。假若让他到齐国都城临淄的闹市上住几年，纵使每天逼迫他说楚国话，也是不可能的。你说薛居州是个好人，让他和君王一起住在王宫里来影响宋王，宋王就会从善。如果王宫里上下都是好人，那宋王又能和谁干坏事呢？如果王宫里上下全是不好的人，那宋王又能和谁做善事呢？一个薛居州就能影响宋王吗？"

七、离娄上篇
Li Lou, Part One

《孟子》之第七篇。孟子提出规矩、方圆和做人的准则。特别是"反求诸己"的修身标准。本篇共 28 章,节选其中 22 章。

孟子对齐宣王说:"规矩是方圆的准则,圣人是做人的准则。作为君王,应尽君王之道;作为臣子,应尽臣子之道。二者只要取法尧和舜就行了。"

7.1 孟子曰:"离娄之明、公输子之巧,不以规矩,不能成方员;师旷之聪,不以六律,不能正五音;尧舜之道,不以仁政,不能平治天下。今有仁心仁闻而民不被其泽,不可法于后世者,不行先王之道也。故曰,徒善不足以为政,徒法不能以自行。

……

"圣人既竭目力焉,继之以规矩准绳,以为方员平直,不可胜用也;既竭耳力焉,继之以六律正五音,不可胜用也;既竭心思焉,继之以不忍人之政,而仁覆天下矣。故曰,为高必因丘陵,为下必因川泽;为政不因先王之道,可谓智乎?是以惟仁者宜在高位。不仁而在高位,是播其恶于众也。上无道揆也，下无法守也，朝不信道，工不信度，君子犯义，小人犯刑，国之所存者幸也。故曰，城郭不完，兵甲不多，非国之灾也；田野不辟，货财不聚，非国之害也。上无礼，下无学，贼民兴，丧无日矣。"

《离娄上篇·1》节选

离娄：相传为黄帝时人，目力极强，能于百步之外看清秋毫之末。**公输子**：名般（一作"班"），鲁国人，又称鲁班。为中国古代著名巧匠。**师旷**：中国古代有名的音乐家，晋平公时任太师（乐官之长）。**六律**：指阳律六。**五音**：中国音阶名，即宫、商、角、徵、羽。

Mencius said, "Even with Li Lou's eyesight and Gongshu Zi's skill, no one can draw a square and a circle without proper tools. Even with Shi Kuang's hearing, no one can check the five notes without the help of the six musical scales. Even with Yao and Shun's statecraft, no one can dominate the world without policies of benevolence. Now some lords do have benevolent hearts and are known for being benevolent, but ordinary people enjoy no benefit from them, so they cannot continue to hold power. The reason would be that they have not ruled according to the way of the sages. So, good politics does not necessarily come about through good intentions, and good methods not come into being by themselves. Since the sages set the standards for circles, squares, levels and straightness first with their eyesight and then with various tools, these standards should be adopted permanently. Since the sages checked the five notes first with their ears and then with the six musical scales, these notes are quite enough for playing all types of music. Since the sages tried their hardest to pursue benevolent policies, benevolence will become the universal morality. Lofty platforms should be built on mountains, deep ponds should be dug in marshes. Would it be wise to run a state without following the ways of the ancient sages? So, only benevolent persons should be in power, or otherwise politics will be in chaos. If the ones high up hold no moral principles, then there will be no law for the ones low down. If the court does not believe in morality and justice, craftsmen will disregard the

◎ 离娄上篇 Li Lou, Part One

rules. If officials break the laws, then ordinary people will do the same. In this way, the state will be in danger. So the main threats to a state are not insecure city walls nor lack of weapons, nor untilled lands and a frail economy. A state will inevitably fall if those high up ignore propriety and righteousness, and those low down are uneducated and undisciplined persons who violate the laws.

Notes: Li Lou: Said to have lived during the reign of the Yellow Emperor. He had such keen eyesight that he could discern the tip of a hair from one hundred feet away.

Gongshu Zi: Also known as Lu Ban, he was a native of Lu and a famous carpenter.

Shi Kuang: Chief musician during the reign of Duke Ping of Jin.

Five notes: The ancient Chinese musical scales—Gong, Shang, Jiao, Zhi and Yu.

孟子说:"即使有离娄的视力,公输般的技巧,如果不借助于工具,也不能画出标准的方形和圆形。即使有师旷那样的审音听力,如果不借助于六律,也不能正确校正五音。即使有尧舜之道,如果不行仁政,也不能平治天下。现在有些诸侯,虽有仁爱之心,也有仁爱的名声,但老百姓却得不到他的一点好处,他的政治也不能延续下去,就是因为他不能实行圣王之道。所以说,光有好心,还不能说就有好的政治。光有好的方法,也不会自己实行起来。

……

"圣人既然已用视力,又借助各种工具造出方的、圆的、平的、直的标准,这些东西就用之不尽了。圣人既然已用听力,又借助六律来校正五音,各种音阶也就运用无穷了。圣人既然用尽心力,实行仁政,那仁便成为天下通行的道德。所以说,筑高台要凭借山陵,挖深池要凑沼泽凹地。如果治理国家不凭借前代圣王之道,那能说是聪明吗?因此,只有仁人才可执政,不仁的人执政,就会把政治搞乱。在上的没有道德规范,在下的就无法可依,朝廷不相信道义,工匠不相信尺度,官吏破坏法度,百姓就会触犯刑法,这样的国家就很危险了。所以说,城墙不坚固,军备不充足,还不是国家最主要的灾难。土地没开辟,经济不富裕,也不是国家主要的祸害。如果在上的人没有礼义,在下的人不受教育,违法乱纪的人都起来了,那国家也就要灭亡了。"

7.2 孟子曰:"规矩,方员之

至也；圣人，人伦之至也。欲为君，尽君道；欲为臣，尽臣道。二者皆法尧舜而已矣。不以舜之所以事尧事君，不敬其君者也；不以尧之所以治民治民，贼其民者也。孔子曰：'道二，仁与不仁而已矣。'暴其民甚，则身弑国亡；不甚，则身危国削，名之曰'幽''厉'，虽孝子慈孙，百世不能改也。诗云：'殷鉴不远，在夏后之世。'此之谓也。"

《离娄上篇·2》

幽、厉：古代帝王、贵族、大臣等死后，依其生前事迹给于的称号叫做谥。据《逸周书·谥法解》曰："动祭乱常曰幽，杀戮无辜曰厉。"可见幽和厉都是恶谥。周朝有周幽王和厉王。

Mencius said, "The compass and the T‑square are the criteria of circles and squares. Sages are the criterion of human relationships. Kings and subjects should strictly observe their proper ways.

Both should take Yao and Shun as their models. To serve one's ruler other than in the way Shun served Yao is to lack respect for him. To govern the ordinary people other than in the way Yao governed the ordinary people is to harm them. Confucius said, 'There are only two ways to run a state: by practicing or not practicing policies of benevolence.' By doing serious harm to the people the ruler brings death on himself and ruin on his kingdom. If the ruler is only a little less harsh, he will still put himself in danger and weaken his kingdom. In that case the king would be given the posthumous title "You" or "Li", which can never be changed even if he has filial and pious descendants. This is just what the *Book of Songs* means when it says, ' Yin had a warning not long ago, from the experience of Xia, which was the previous dynasty.' "

Note: You and Li: In ancient times posthumous titles were given to emperors, nobles and ministers according to their behavior in their lifetimes. According to the *Yi Zhou Shu: Interpretation of Posthumous Titles*, the title *You* was given to the deceased if he did not observe the proper way during his lifetime, and *Li* was awarded if he slaughtered innocent people. So both *You* and *Li* are derogatory titles. Zhou Dynasty had two emperors awarded the titles *You* and *Li*, respectively.

孟子说:"规矩是方圆的准则,圣人是做人的准则。作为君主,应尽君主之道;作为臣子,应尽臣子之道。二者只要取法尧和舜就行了。不以舜事尧的态度和方法服事君主,便是对君主的不敬;君主不以尧治理百姓的态度和方法治理百姓,便是害民。孔子说:'治理国家的方法有两种,行仁政和不行仁政罢了。'害民政治,重则身亡国灭;轻则身危国弱。死后谥之为'幽'、'厉',纵使他有孝子顺孙,历百代也更改不了。《诗经》上说过,'殷商有一面离它不远的镜子,就是前一代的夏朝。'说的正是这个意思。"

7.3 孟子曰:"三代之得天下也以仁,其失天下也以不仁。国之所以废兴存亡者亦然。天子不仁,不保四海;诸侯不仁,不保社稷;卿大夫不仁,不保宗庙;士庶人不仁,不保四体。今恶死亡而乐不仁,是犹恶醉而强酒。"

《离娄上篇·3》

Mencius said, "The three dynasties, Xia, Shang and Zhou, could dominate the world because they all practiced policies of benevolence, and they lost their empires because they all discarded policies of benevolence. The prosperity and decay of kingdoms also follow this rule. Emperors can not keep their empires if they are not benevolent; kings cannot keep their kingdoms if they are not benevolent; ministers cannot keep their manors if they are not benevolent and scholars and ordinary people cannot keep their lives if they are not benevolent. Now there are men who detest death but love cruelty. This is like detesting drunkenness but continuing to drink."

孟子说:"夏、商、周三代以仁得天下,以不仁失天下。国家的兴盛和衰亡也是这个道理。天子不仁,便不能保全天下;诸侯不仁,便不能保全国家;卿大夫不仁,便不能保全封地;士人和老百姓不仁,便不能保全自身。现在有些人怕死,却又不仁,这好比怕醉却偏要喝酒一样。"

7.4 孟子曰:"爱人不亲,反其仁;治人不治,反其智;礼人不答,反其敬——行有不得者皆反求诸己,其身正而天下归之。诗云:'永言配命,自求多福。'"

《离娄上篇·4》

Mencius said, "When one loves but fails to receive love in return, one should reflect on whether one is really a benevolent man. When one fails to subject others to discipline, one should reflect on whether one knows the proper way to govern. When one fails to gain respect from others while treating others with the proper courtesies, one should reflect on whether one is sincere enough. One should reflect on oneself whenever one fails to get the expected results. If a ruler behaves correctly, all the people will pay allegiance to him. The *Book of Songs* says, 'The Zhou reign was long because it conformed to Heaven's will. Be strict with oneself and blessings will descend.'"

孟子说:"爱别人,却得不到别人的爱,就要反问自己是否真正有仁爱之心。管理别人,却没有管理好,就要反省自己的管理方法是否正确,知识是否够用。以礼待人却得不到别人的尊重,就要反责自己对别人的态度是否真诚。任何行为如果没有得到预期的效果都要反躬自责,自己的确端正了,天下人便会归向他。《诗经》上说:'周朝久远是天意,严格自身才能多福。'"

7.5 孟子曰:"人有恒言,皆曰,'天下国家。'天下之本在国,国之本在家,家之本在身。"

《离娄上篇·5》

天下国家:孟子所说天下即指中国,国即指中国境内的各诸侯国。故儒家认为"身修而后家齐,家齐而后国治,国治而后天下平"(《礼记·大学》)。

Mencius said, "There is a common saying about 'the empire, kingdoms and families'. Kingdoms are the basis of the empire, families are the basis of a kingdom and individuals are the basis of a family."

Note: "The empire" here refers to China. "Kingdoms" refers to the feudal states within the boundaries of China. Confucians advocated "Good family is based on the cultivation of oneself; administration of a kingdom is based on good families, and unification of the empire is based on the administration of kingdoms". (The *Book of Rites*, *The Great Learning*)

孟子说:"人们常说'天下国家'这句话,可见天下的基础是国,国的基础是家,家的基础是人。"

7.7 孟子曰:"天下有道,小德役大德,小贤役大贤;天下无道,小役大,弱役强。斯二者,天也。顺天者存,逆天者亡。"

《离娄上篇·7》节选

Mencius said, "When the world is in good order, people of low morality listen to people of high morality, and ordinary people listen to persons of virtue. When the world is in chaos, the powerful enslave the powerless, the strong enslave the weak.

In both cases, the will of Heaven prevails. Those who follow Heaven's will survive and those who disobey Heaven's will perish."

孟子说:"国家政治清明,道德低的人听命于道德高的人,一般人听命于贤人。国家政治黑暗,力量大的奴役力量小的,强的奴役弱的。这两种情况都是由天命决定的。顺从天命者生存,违背天命者灭亡。"

7.8 孟子曰:"不仁者可与言哉?安其危而利其菑,乐其所以亡者。不仁而可与言,则何亡国败家之有?有孺子歌曰:'沧浪之水清兮,可以濯我缨;沧浪之水浊兮,可以濯我足。'孔子曰:'小子听之!清斯濯缨,浊斯濯足矣。自取之也。'夫人必自侮,然后人侮之;家必自毁,而后人毁之;国必自伐,而后人伐之。太甲曰:'天作孽,犹可违;自作孽,不可活。'此之谓也。"

《离娄上篇·8》

Mencius said, "How can one be a colleague to unbenevolent persons? They remain indifferent when they see others in difficulties and dangers. What they aspire to is the happiness and enjoyments which bring disasters to kingdoms and families. If such persons can be one's colleagues, why are there disasters to kingdoms and families? A children's song goes, 'I wash my hat and tassels in clean water and wash my feet in dirty water.' Confucius said, 'Be sure to wash your hats and tassels in clean water and your feet in dirty water. The nature of the water determines this.' So a person can only be insulted when his own behavior invites insults; a family will be destroyed only when it has destroyed itself beforehand, and a kingdom will be invaded only when it provides a cause. This is what the *Book of History* means when it says, 'Natural disasters can be avoided, but not punishment for one's bad conduct.'"

孟子说:"难道可以和不仁的人共事吗?他

们看见别人处于危难之中，却无动于衷，甚至幸灾乐祸。他们追求的是足以亡国败家的欢乐。如果不仁的人也可以共事，那怎么会发生亡国败家的事呢？从前有首儿歌唱道：'清沏的水可以洗我的帽缨，混浊的水可以洗我的脚。'孔子说：'学生们记住，水清就洗帽缨，水浊就洗脚，这是由水本身决定的。'所以，人必先有遭侮辱的行为，才会遭别人侮辱；家必先有毁坏的因素，外力才能毁坏它；国必先有被讨伐的原因，才会被别国讨伐。《尚书·太甲篇》上说：'天灾尚可逃避，自己作孽是逃不过惩罚的。'正是这个意思。"

7.9 孟子曰："桀纣之失天下也，失其民也；失其民者，失其心也。得天下有道：得其民，斯得天下矣；得其民有道：得其心，斯得民矣；得其心有道：所欲与之聚之，所恶勿施，尔也。民之归仁也，犹水之就下、兽之走圹也。"

《离娄上篇·9》节选

Mencius said, "The reason Jie and Zhou failed to keep their empires is that they had lost the support and confidence of their people. So the way to win the world is to win the support and confidence of the people, and the way to win the support and confidence of the people is to do what will benefit the people and undo what the people detest. People will submit to policies of benevolence as water flows downhill and animals gather in deserted land and forests."

孟子说:"夏桀和商纣丧失天下的原因,是由于失去了百姓的支持,失去了民心。所以,得天下的方法在于得到百姓的支持,获得民心,而获得民心的方法只有多干对百姓有利的事,不干百姓厌恶的事。百姓归附于仁政,好像水往低处流,野兽向旷野山林一样。"

7.10 孟子曰:"自暴者,不可与有言也;自弃者,不可与有为也。言非礼义,谓之自暴也;吾身不能居仁由义,谓之自弃也。仁,人之安宅也;义,人之正路也。旷安宅而弗居，舍正路而不由，哀哉！"

《离娄上篇·10》

Mencius said, "One may not converse with someone who does violence to himself, and one may not cooperate with someone who has abandoned himself. To say anything against propriety and righteousness is to do violence to oneself; to think oneself incapable of practicing benevolence and justice is to look down upon oneself. Benevolence is where one should reside; justice is the right road along which one should go. It is a pity to refuse to reside where one should reside and depart from the road one should follow!"

孟子说："和糟蹋自己的人，谈不出什么有益的话；和瞧不起自己的人，干不成什么大事。出言破坏礼义，就是自己糟蹋自己，认为自己不能行仁义，就是自己瞧不起自己。仁是人应居之处，义是人之正路。舍应居之处不居，舍正道不走，乃是人之悲哀。"

7.11 孟子曰:"道在迩而求诸远,事在易而求诸难:人人亲其亲、长其长,而天下平。"

《离娄上篇·11》

Mencius said, "One walks from the near to the distant and starts with the easy and moves on to the difficult. If one loves his parents and respects his seniors, the world will be at peace."

孟子说:"走路由近及远,做事由易及难。只要人人能亲爱自己的双亲,尊敬自己的长辈,天下就会太平。"

7.12 孟子曰:"居下位而不获于上,民不可得而治也。获于上有道,不信于友,弗获于上矣。信于友有道,事亲弗悦,弗信于友矣。悦亲有道,反身不诚,不悦于亲矣。诚身有道,不明乎善,不诚其身矣。是故诚者,天之道也;思诚者，人之道也。至诚而不动者，未之有也；不诚，未有能动者也。"

《离娄上篇·12》

Mencius said,"A man of low degree who cannot win the confidence of his superiors cannot govern the people well. To win the confidence of his superiors, he should be able to win the confidence of his friends first. How can he win the confidence of his superiors if he cannot win the confidence of his friends? To win the confidence of his friends, he should be able to please his parents first. If he cannot please his parents, he will not be able to win the confidence of his friends. To please his parents, he should serve them with sincerity. How can he please his parents if he is insincere when he reflects on himself? To become sincere, one has to be certain what is good. One cannot be sincere if one does not know what is good. So, sincerity is a natural course and pursuit of sincerity is the criterion of behavior. With sincerity, no one will not be moved; without sincerity, no one will be moved."

孟子说:"职位低又得不到上级信任的人,是不能管好百姓的。要想得到上级的信任,首先要得到朋友的信任,如果连朋友都不信任你,又怎能得到上级信任呢?要使朋友信任你,首先要使父母满意,如果侍奉父母而不能使父母满意,也就不会得到朋友的信任。要使父母满意,首先侍奉父母要心诚。反躬自责,若自己心意不诚,又怎能使父母满意呢?要使自己心诚,首先要明白什么是善,若不明白什么是善,也就不能使自己心诚了。所以诚是自然的规律,追求诚是做人的准则。没有心诚而不能感动别人的,也没有心不诚而能感动别人的。"

7.14 孟子曰:"求也为季氏宰,无能改于其德,而赋粟倍他日。孔子曰:'求非我徒也,小子鸣鼓而攻之可也。'由此观之,君不行仁政而富之,皆弃于孔子者也,况于为之强战?争地以战,杀人盈野;争城以战,杀人盈城。此所谓率土地而食人肉,罪不容于死。故善战者服上刑,连诸侯者次之，辟草莱、任土地者次之。"

《离娄上篇·14》

求：冉求，即子有。孔子的学生。当时是季孙氏家臣。季孙氏要利用改变田赋制度来增加税收，派冉求征求孔子的意见，孔子明确表示反对对老百姓的过分剥削。可是冉求仍然听从季氏而实行新的田赋制度加重对人民的剥削，所以孔子不认他这个学生，并号召其他学生攻击他。

Mencius said, "Ran Qiu was an aide to Ji Sun, a high official of Lu. But instead of advising his lord to reduce the farm tax, he got him to double it. Confucius said, 'He is no longer a disciple of mine. He may be openly criticized.' From this, we can discern that Confucius detested those who helped unbenevolent persons in power to amass wealth, not to mention those who actually fight for such unbenevolent persons. They would help unbenevolent masters to seize land, filling the fields with the bodies of the slain. They would also help their unbenevolent masters to occupy cities, filling them up with the bodies of the slain. This is what is called killing for the sake of amassing land. Death is too good a punishment for such people. So the bellicose should be executed, those who plot aggressive alliances should be given punishment in the second degree and those who force ordinary people to open up wasteland in order to squeeze more wealth out of them should be given punishment in the third degree."

Note：Qiu：Ran Qiu, also named Zi You, a disciple of Confucius. His master Ji Sun wanted to increase his tax revenue by changing the land tax system, and so sent Ran Qiu to seek advice from Confucius. The latter was firmly against over-exploitation of ordinary people and would not recognize Ran Qiu as his disciple. He called on his other disciples to criticize Ran Qiu for obeying Ji Sun's instruction to adopt the new land taxation system.

孟子说："冉求做鲁国大夫季孙氏的家臣，却不能改变他增收赋税的行为，把田赋增加了一倍。孔子说：'冉求已经不是我的学生，你们可以大张旗鼓地攻击他。'从这看来，执政者不行仁政，那些反而去帮助他聚敛财富的人，是被孔子所唾弃的，更何况那些替不仁的执政者而卖命的人呢？这些人为执政者争夺土地而战，杀人遍野。为争夺城池而战，杀人满城。这就是为聚敛土地而致人于死地，这种人罪不容诛。

所以对好战者应处以重刑，对从事合纵连横游学的人处以次一等的刑罚，对为了聚敛财富迫使老百姓开垦荒地的人处以再次一等的刑罚。"

7.15 孟子曰："存乎人者，莫良于眸子。眸子不能掩其恶。胸中正，则眸子瞭焉；胸中不正，则眸子眊焉。听其言也，观其眸子，人焉廋哉？"

《离娄上篇·15》

Mencius said, "To know a person, there is no better way than to look straight into his eyes, because the eyes can never conceal evil. One has bright eyes if one has a clear conscience, but the eyes are cloudy if one harbors evil intentions. Look straight into his eyes while listening to his words, and he won't be able to conceal what is in his mind."

孟子说："观察一个人，没有比观察他的眼睛更准确了。因为眼睛不能掩盖一个人的丑恶。心正，则眼睛明亮；心不正，则目不明。听一个人说话的时候，注意观察他的眼睛，这个人的善恶是无法隐藏的。"

7.16 孟子曰："恭者不侮人，俭者不夺人。侮夺人之君，惟恐不顺焉，恶得为恭俭？恭俭岂可以声音笑貌为哉？"

《离娄上篇·16》

Mencius said, "A courteous man will not insult others; a self-restrained man will not rob others. How can a ruler become courteous and restrained when he insults and robs others all the time lest they should not be obedient to him? Courtesy and restraint are more than mere nice words and smiles."

孟子说："有礼貌的人不会侮辱别人，节俭的人不会掠夺别人。有些诸侯，一味侮辱别人，掠夺别人，唯恐别人不顺从自己，怎么能做到有礼貌和节俭呢？有礼貌和节俭这两种品德不是可以凭好听的言语和笑脸做得出来的。"

7.17 淳于髡曰:"男女授受不亲,礼与?"孟子曰:"礼也。"曰:"嫂溺,则援之以手乎?"曰:"嫂溺不援,是豺狼也。男女授受不亲,礼也;嫂溺,援之以手者,权也。"曰:"今天下溺矣,夫子之不援,何也?"曰:"天下溺,援之以道;嫂溺,援之以手——子欲手援天下乎?"

《离娄上篇·17》

Chunyu Kun asked, "Is it ordained in the rites that males and females should not make physical contact?" Mencius said, "Yes."

Chunyu Kun said, "But what if your sister-in-law were drowning and you extended your hand to save her?"

Mencius said, "A man would be no better than an animal if he did not. The rites do indeed forbid physical contact between males and females. But in the case of a drowning sister-in-law the rites allow a man to extend a hand to save her."

Chunyu Kun said, "Now all the people in the world are drowning; why don't you save them?"

Mencius said, "If all the people of the world are drowning they are to be saved by means of the Tao. A drowning sister-in-law is to be saved with the hand. Do you expect me to save all the people in the world with my hand?"

Note:

Chunyu Kun: Chunyu is his surname and Kun his name. He was a man of the State of Qi and served kings Wei, Xuan and Hui.

淳于髡问:"男女之间,授受不亲,这是礼制吗?"孟子回答说:"是礼制。"

淳于髡说:"那么,假如眼看着嫂嫂掉到水里,可以用手去拉她吗?"

孟子说:"看见嫂嫂掉到水里,不去拉她,这简直是豺狼。男女之间授受不亲,这是常礼。看见嫂嫂掉到水里,用手去救她,这是变通的办法。"

淳于髡说:"现在天下人都掉在了水里,您不去救援,又是什么缘故呢?"

孟子说:"天下人都掉在水里了,要用'道'去援救;嫂嫂掉在水里,用手去援救——

你难道要我用一双手去援救天下人吗？"

淳于髡：姓淳于，名髡，齐国人。曾仕于齐威王、宣王和惠王之朝。

7.18 公孙丑曰："君子之不教子，何也？"

孟子曰："势不行也。教者必以正；以正不行，继之以怒。继之以怒，则反夷矣。'夫子教我以正，夫子未出于正也。'则是父子相夷也。父子相夷，则恶矣。古者易子而教之，父子之间不责善。责善则离，离则不祥莫大焉。"

《离娄上篇·18》

Gongsun Chou said, "Generally, a gentleman does not teach his own son. Why?"

Mencius said, "Because it won't work. Education must be conducted in the right way. One gets angry when such a way does not work. Once one gets angry, it hurts others' feelings. The son would say, 'You say education must be conducted in the right way, but your behavior does not conform to what you teach me.' In this way, father and son would become estranged, and this is not right. In ancient times gentlemen exchanged sons to educate them, in order to avoid mutual blaming. Mutual blaming would lead to estrangement, which is the worst thing in the world."

公孙丑问:"君子一般不亲自教自己的儿子,这是什么道理?"

孟子说:"由于情势行不通。教育一定要用正理正道,这样教育无效的时候,就容易发怒。一发怒,就会伤害感情。儿子会说:'您用正理正道教我,可您的行为却不符合正理正道。'这就伤了父子间的感情。父子间伤感情是很不好的。古时候君子往往互相交换儿子来教育,使父子间避免发生冲突,父子间发生冲突,就容易产生隔阂,父子间产生隔阂,是君子最伤脑筋的事。"

7.19 孟子曰:"事,孰为大?事亲为大;守,孰为大?守身为大。不失其身而能事其亲者，吾闻之矣；失其身而能事其亲者，吾未之闻也。孰不为事？事亲，事之本也；孰不为守？守身，守之本也。"

《离娄上篇·19》节选

Mencius said, "Whom should be served first? Parents should be served first. What should be kept first? Moral integrity should be kept first. I have heard that there are people who can both keep their moral integrity and revere their parents, but I have never heard of anyone who can lose his moral integrity but revere his parents. There are many persons one should support, but supporting one's parents is the base. There are many things that should be kept, but keeping moral integrity is the base."

孟子说："侍奉谁最重要？侍奉父母最重要。守护什么最重要？守护自己的节操最重要。不丧失自己的操守，又能侍奉父母的人，我听说过。已丧失自己的操守，却能侍奉父母的人，我没有听说过。侍奉的事都应该做，但侍奉父母是根本。守护的事都应该做,但守护自己的节操是根本。"

7.20 孟子曰:"君仁,莫不仁;君义,莫不义;君正,莫不正。一正君而国定矣。"

《离娄上篇·20》节选

Mencius said, "If rulers are benevolent, then all their people will be benevolent too. If rulers are righteous, then all their people will be righteous also. If rulers are upright, all their people will be upright also. When rulers' errors are corrected their kingdoms will be stable."

孟子说:"君主仁,没有人不仁。君主义,没有人不义。君主正,没有人不正。只要把君主端正了,国家就安定了。"

7.21 孟子曰:"有不虞之誉,有求全之毁。"

《离娄上篇·21》

Mencius said, "There is unexpected praise and highly demanding censure."

孟子说:"有意想不到的赞誉,也有过于苛求的诋毁。"

7.22 孟子曰:"人之易其言也,无责耳矣。"

《离娄上篇·22》

Mencius said, "Those who indulge themselves in verbiage will have no achievements."

孟子说:"夸夸其谈的人,不足以任大事。"

7.23 孟子曰:"人之患在好为人师。"

《离娄上篇·23》

Mencius said, "The trouble with people is that they are just too eager to assume the role of teacher."

孟子说:"人最怕总喜欢做人家的老师。"

7.27 孟子曰:"仁之实,事亲是也;义之实,从兄是也;智之实,知斯二者弗去是也;礼之实,节文斯二者是也;乐之实,乐斯二者,乐则生矣;生则恶可已也,恶可已,则不知足之蹈之手之舞之。"

《离娄上篇·27》

Mencius said, "The core of benevolence is to be filial to one's parents; the core of righteousness is to yield to one's elder brothers; the core of wisdom is to know the meaning of benevolence and righteousness and adhere to them steadfastly, the core of propriety is to regulate and adjust the relations between benevolence and righteousness; the core of happiness is the enjoyment of practicing benevolence and righteousness. Once happiness begins, there is no end to it, and one will unconsciously dance to express one's happiness."

孟子说:"仁的核心是孝顺父母;义的核心是顺从兄长;智的核心是明白仁和义的道理而坚持不懈;礼的核心是能对仁和义加以调节和修饰;乐的核心是能从实行仁和义中得到快乐;快乐一发生就无法休止,无法休止就会不知不觉地手舞足蹈起来了。"

八、离娄下篇
Li Lou, Part Two

《孟子》之第八篇。孟子讲善与人性,君与臣及"仁者爱人"的道理。本篇共33章,节选其中23章。

孟子给弟子们讲子产的故事。说从前有人给子产送条活鱼,子产让管理池塘的人把鱼放进池塘养起来。那人却把鱼煮吃了,还欺骗子产说已经把鱼放进了池塘,子产相信了他,很高兴。孟子讲完故事又说:"对君子,可以用合乎情理的方法欺骗他,却不能用违反道德的诡诈来迷惘他。"

8.2 子产听郑国之政,以其乘舆济人于溱洧。孟子曰:"惠而不知为政。岁十一月,徒杠成;十二月,舆梁成,民未病涉也。君子平其政,行辟人可也,焉得人人而济之?故为政者,每人而悦之,日亦不足矣。"

《离娄下篇·2》

子产:春秋时郑国贤相公孙侨,字子产。溱、洧:皆水名。

When Zichan was in charge of the government of the State of Zheng, he helped people cross the Zhen and Wei rivers using his own carriage. Mencius said, "He was kind but he knew nothing about politics. If he had repaired the bridge in advance, people would have had no trouble crossing those rivers. So long as the ruler runs the state well, he can shoo the people out of his way. There is no need to help them cross flooded rivers one by one. That way he would not have enough time to win everyone's favor."

Notes: Zichan: Gongsun Qiao, a noted prime minister of the State of Zheng in the Spring and Autumn Period.

Zhen, Wei: Names of rivers.

子产治理郑国时,曾用自己所乘车子帮助别人渡河。孟子说:"这不过是小恩小惠,其实他并不懂政治。如果提前把桥修好,老百姓就不会为渡河发愁了。执政者只要把国家治理好,他外出尽可以鸣锣开道,哪里用得着去帮助别人一个一个渡河呢?如果执政者去讨每个人的欢心,那时间就太不够用了。"

8.3 孟子告齐宣王曰:"君之视臣如手足,则臣视君如腹心;君之视臣如犬马,则臣视君如国人;君之视臣如土芥,则臣视君如寇仇。"

《离娄下篇·3》节选

Mencius said to King Xuan of Qi: "If a king treats his ministers as his hands and feet, his ministers will treat him as their hearts and bellies. If a king treats his ministers like dogs and horses, his ministers will treat him as a commoner. If a king treats his ministers as soil and trash, his ministers will treat him as an enemy."

孟子对齐宣王说:"君主视臣下如手足,臣下就会视君主如腹心;君主视臣下如狗马,臣下就会视君主如常人;君主视臣下如泥土草芥,臣下就会视君主如仇敌。"

8.5 孟子曰:"君仁,莫不仁;君义,莫不义。"

《离娄下篇·5》

Mencius said, "No one will be unkind if the king is benevolent, and no one will be unrighteous if the king is just."

孟子说:"君主仁,则无人不仁。君主义,则无人不义。"

8.6 孟子曰:"非礼之礼,非

义之义，大人弗为。"

《离娄下篇·6》

Mencius said, "A man of virtue will not observe specious rites, nor will he administer specious justice."

孟子说："似是而非的礼，似是而非的义，道德高尚的人是不干的。"

8.7 孟子曰："中也养不中，才也养不才，故人乐有贤父兄也。如中也弃不中，才也弃不才，则贤不肖之相去，其间不能以寸。"

《离娄下篇·7》

Mencius said, "Men of lofty morality should educate and influence men of doubtful morality; men of talent should educate and influence untalented men. For everyone delights in having a talented and highly moral superior. If men of lofty morality do not educate and influence men of doubtful morality and men of talent do not educate and influence untalented men, then good cannot be distinguished from bad."

孟子说:"道德高尚的人来教育影响道德不高的人,才能高的人来教育影响才能低下的人,所以每个人都希望有个才德高尚的长者。如果道德高尚的人不去教育影响道德不高的人,才能高的人不去教育影响才能低下的人,那么,就无所谓差别了。"

8.8 孟子曰:"人有不为也,而后可以有为。"

《离娄下篇·8》

Mencius said, "A person can make some achievement only when there is something that he does not do."

孟子说:"人要有所不为,才能有所为。"

8.9 孟子曰:"言人之不善,当如后患何?"

《离娄下篇·9》

Mencius said, "What shall a man do when he meets with some misfortune in the future if he talks about others' shortcomings now?"

孟子说:"尽说别人的坏话,日后祸患来了,自己怎么办呢?"

8.11 孟子曰:"大人者,言不必信,行不必果,惟义所在。"

《离娄下篇·11》

Mencius said, "A man of virtue need not keep his word and act resolutely all the time so long as all his words and actions conform to the right course."

孟子说:"有德行的人,说话不一定句句守信,行为不一定事事决断,其言行只要符合义就行。"

8.12 孟子曰:"大人者,不失其赤子之心者也。"

《离娄下篇·12》

Mencius said, "A man of virtue is one who has a heart as innocent as that of a new-born babe."

孟子说:"道德高尚的人就是能保持纯洁善良之心的人。"

8.14 孟子曰:"君子深造之以道,欲其自得之也。自得之,则居之安;居之安,则资之深;资之深,则取之左右逢其原,故君子欲其自得之也。"

《离娄下篇·14》

Mencius said, "A gentleman should advance his study in correct ways so as to acquire knowledge by himself. Once he does so, he is able to master it firmly. Firm mastery of knowledge leads to a rich accumulation of knowledge, and the use of it will be inexhaustible. So a gentleman goes all out to acquire knowledge by himself."

孟子说:"君子深造必以正确的方法,使自

己有所体会。自有所得，就能牢固掌握。牢固掌握，就能积蓄深厚。积蓄深厚，便能取之不尽，左右逢源，所以君子要强调自己有所体会。"

8.15 孟子曰："博学而详说之，将以反说约也。"

《离娄下篇·15》

Mencius said, "Learn extensively, expound in detail and explain the cardinal principles briefly on the basis of mastery of knowledge."

孟子说："广博地学习，详细地解说，在融会贯通的基础上再简略地述说大义。"

8.16 孟子曰："以善服人者，未有能服人者也；以善养人，然后能服天下。天下不心服而王者，未之有也。"

《离娄下篇·16》

Mencius said, "One can never convince others

with truth, but all the world will be convinced if one educates the world with truth. One can never unify the world if the hearts of all the people are not won over."

孟子说:"以善服人,没有能使人服从的。以善教人,能使天下人归服。从来没有天下人心不服而能统一天下的。"

8.17 孟子曰:"言无实不祥。不祥之实,蔽贤者当之。"

《离娄下篇·17》

Mencius said, "It is not right to utter empty words; empty words come from those who stifle criticism and suggestions."

孟子说:"言之无物是不好的,这是由堵塞贤路者造成的。"

8.18 徐子曰:"仲尼亟称于水,曰'水哉,水哉!'何取于水也?"孟子曰:"源泉混混,不舍昼夜，盈科而后进，放乎四海。有本者如是，是之取尔。苟为无本，七八月之间雨集，沟浍皆盈；其涸也，可立而待也。故声闻过情，君子耻之。"

《离娄下篇·18》

徐子：孟子弟子徐辟。

Xu Zi said, "Confucius praised water highly, saying, 'Ah, water! Ah, water!' What quality of water did he praise?"

Mencius said, "Gurgling water flows from its source day and night, covering the low land and pouring into the seas and oceans. What Confucius praised was the fact that water has its source. If water had no source, it would flood the ditches in the rainy season, but would dry up in no time. Thus is why a gentleman is ashamed of his reputation surpassing his qualities."

Note：Xu Zi：Xu Pi, a disciple of Mencius.

孟子弟子徐辟说:"孔子曾数次称赞水,总说'水呀,水呀!'他到底称赞水什么呢?"

孟子说:"有源之水汩汩而流,昼夜不停,漫过坎地,奔流向前,一直注入海洋。孔子就是赞扬水之有源这一点。假如是无源之水,一到雨季就沟渠盈满,但很快就干枯了。所以君子以名不副实为耻。"

8.19　孟子曰:"人之所以异于禽兽者几希,庶民去之,君子存之。舜明于庶物,察于人伦,由仁义行,非行仁义也。"

《离娄下篇·19》

Mencius said, "There is not much difference between human beings and animals. Common people ignore the difference; gentlemen realize and retain the difference. Shun knew the difference so he practiced policies of benevolence and righteousness and did not take them as a means only."

孟子说:"人和禽兽的区别只有很少一点,一般百姓不重视它,只有君子才保存它。舜懂得这一点，于是行仁义却不把仁义当作工具手段来使用。"

8.20 孟子曰："禹恶旨酒而好善言。汤执中，立贤无方。文王视民如伤，望道而未之见。武王不泄迩，不忘远。周公思兼三王，以施四事；其有不合者，仰而思之，夜以继日；幸而得之，坐以待旦。"

《离娄下篇·20》

Mencius said, "Yu preferred truth to good wine. Tang adhered to the doctrine of the mean and promoted men of virtue without regard to their class background. King Wen treated and consoled ordinary people as if they were physically hurt, and never ceased to pursue truth. King Wu valued ministers in the court but did not forget the lords outside the court. Duke Zhou wished to learn from the kings of the Xia, Shang and Zhou dynasties so as to carry out the achievements of Yu, Tang, Wen and Wu. If any of his behaviors did not conform to reality, he would sit up days and nights pondering the matter. Once he had the solution, he would put it into practice immediately."

孟子说:"禹不好美酒,而好真理。汤坚持中正之道,选择贤人不拘一格。文王对待百姓像对受伤者一样加以抚慰,并不断追求真理。武王尊重朝臣,不忘诸侯。周公想要兼学夏、商、周三代的君王,来实践禹、汤、文王、武王的勋业。有不合现实的情况,日夜苦思冥想,一旦想通,马上付诸实行。"

8.22 孟子曰:"君子之泽五世而斩,小人之泽五世而斩。予未得为孔子徒也,予私淑诸人也。"

《离娄下篇·22》

Mencius said, "The influence of a gentleman on posterity lasts five generations only, as does that of a petty man. I was born too late to be a disciple of Confucius; I learned from other virtuous men."

孟子说:"君子对后世的影响五代就会衰亡,小人对后世的影响五代以后也会消失。我没能够做孔子的门徒,我是自己向诸贤人学习来的。"

8.23 孟子曰:"可以取,可以无取,取伤廉;可以与,可以无与,与伤惠;可以死,可以无死,死伤勇。"

《离娄下篇·23》

伤惠、伤勇:过去一般人认为:"可以与,可以无与,则宜与;可以死,可以无死,则宜死。"孟子却反其道,提出"与伤惠,死伤勇。"意思是恩惠不是指小恩小惠,勇敢不是轻生。

Mencius said, "It would be corruption to take if one could choose between 'to take' and 'not to take'. It would not be a favor to give if one could choose between 'to give' and 'not to give'. It would not be courage to die if one could choose between 'to die' and 'not to die'."

Note: "Not be a favor" and "not be courage": It was a common idea that one should give if one could choose between giving and not giving, and one should die if one could choose between dying and not dying. But Mencius thought otherwise. He suggested that it would not be a favor to give and it would not be courage to die, because favor does not mean petty favor and courage does not mean making light of one's life.

孟子说:"可取可不取,取则有损廉洁。可给可不给,给则有损恩惠。可死可不死,死则有损勇敢。"

8.25 孟子曰:"西子蒙不洁,则人皆掩鼻而过之;虽有恶人,齐戒沐浴,则可以祀上帝。"

《离娄下篇·25》

西子:古代美女西施。

Mencius said, "If Xi Zi were covered in filth, everyone would pass her by holding his nose. If an ugly man fasts and bathes he may offer sacrifices to the Lord of Heaven."

Note: Xi Zi: Also named Xi Shi, the archetypal beauty of ancient times.

孟子说:"如果西施满身肮脏,别人也会掩鼻而过;纵是面貌丑陋的人,如果斋戒沐浴,也可以祭祀上帝。"

8.26 孟子曰:"天下之言性也,则故而已矣。故者以利为本。所恶于智者,为其凿也。如智者若禹之行水也,则无恶于智矣。禹之行水也,行其所无事也。如智者亦行其所无事,则智亦大矣。天之高也,星辰之远也,苟求其故,千岁之日至,可坐而致也。"

《离娄下篇·26》

Mencius said, "When one talks about the nature of something, he needs to know how it comes to be what it is, and the key to knowing how it comes to be what it is is to see how it functions. We detest those who claim to be intelligent because they tend to make strained interpretations of things. If they behaved in the same way as Yu regulated the waterways, we would not detest them. The way Yu regulated the waterways was to allow them to go their own ways and to dredge them according to the circumstances. Intelligent men would be all the more intelligent if they could let everything go its own way. Though the sky is extremely lofty and the stars extremely far away, if only one knew how they come to be what they are one could calculate the solar terms of one thousand years hence."

孟子说:"天下人论本性,只要能知道其所以然就行了。推求其所以然的基础是顺其自然之理。我们所以厌恶使用聪明这个词,是因为这个词容易陷于穿凿附会。假如是指像禹治水那样的人,就不会厌恶这个词了。禹治水,就是顺其自然,因势利导。假如聪明人也能这样,那真是很聪明的了。天高星远,只要能推知其所以然,一千年后的节日也能推算出来。"

8.28 孟子曰:"君子所以异于人者,以其存心也。君子以仁存心,以礼存心。仁者爱人,有礼者敬人。爱人者,人恒爱之;敬人者，人恒敬之。""若夫君子所患则亡矣。非仁无为也，非礼无行也。如有一朝之患，则君子不患矣。"

《离娄下篇·28》节选

Mencius said, "A gentleman differs from ordinary people in that he has different ideas in his mind. What he has in his mind is benevolence and the rites. A benevolent person loves others and a polite man respects others. The ones who love others will always be loved by others and the one who respect others will always be respected by others."
Mencius said, "A gentleman has nothing to worry about so long as he does not do anything unkind or contrary to the rites. Then if disaster should strike out of the blue he will be unscathed."

孟子说："君子和一般人不同的地方，就在于心里想的不一样。君子心里想的是仁，是礼。仁人爱人，有礼的人懂得恭敬别人。爱别人的人，别人也会爱他。恭敬别人的人，别人也会恭敬他。"

孟子说："君子别的忧虑是没有的。不干不

仁的事，不做无礼的事。即使一旦有意外的祸患突然降临，君子也不以为痛苦的，因为君子问心无愧。"

8.32 储子曰："王使人瞯夫子，果有以异于人乎？"孟子曰："何以异于人哉？尧舜与人同耳。"

《离娄下篇·32》

Chuzi, the prime minister of the State of Qi, said, "Someone has been sent by the king to spy on you. Are you really different from other men?" Mencius said, "Not at all! Even Yao and Shun were both like ordinary people."

齐相储子对孟子说："王曾派人窥探您，您真有和别人不同的地方吗？"

孟子说："有什么不同呢？尧、舜也同一般人一样呢。"

8.33 齐人有一妻一妾而处室者，其良人出，则必餍酒肉而后反。其妻问所与饮食者，则尽富贵也。其妻告其妾曰:"良人出,则必餍酒肉而后反;问其与饮食者,尽富贵也,而未尝有显者来,吾将瞷良人之所之也。"蚤起,施从良人之所之,遍国中无与立谈者。卒之东郭墦间,之祭者,乞其馀;不足,又顾而之他——此其为餍足之道也。其妻归,告其妾,曰:"良人者,所仰望而终身也,今若此——"与其妾讪其良人,而相泣于中庭,而良人未之知也,施施从外来,骄其妻妾。

由君子观之,则人之所以求富贵利达者,其妻妾不羞也,而不相泣者,几希矣。

《离娄下篇·33》

A certain man of Qi had a wife and a concubine. Whenever he came back home, he had always eaten and drunk his fill. When his wife asked him with whom he had been spending his time, he always named rich and powerful men. His wife said to his concubine: "Every time our husband comes home he has always eaten and drunk his fill. When I ask him with whom he has been spending his time, he always names rich and powerful men. But no man of high rank has ever visited us. I am going to spy on him and see where he goes." The next morning she followed her husband out and saw that no one in the city spoke to him. When they came to a graveyard in the eastern suburb she saw her husband beg for what was left over from a funeral sacrifice. When he did not get enough, he went away to other places to beg. This was the way he managed to eat and drink his fill every day.

When the wife got back home, she told the concubine what she had seen, and said, "Our husband is the person upon whom we depend. Who would have thought...?" When they both were weeping and cursing their husband in the courtyard he returned and, ignoring their distress, treated them with the utmost haughtiness.

In the gentleman's view, there are few who can seek rank and riches without making their wives and concubines feel ashamed and weep.

齐国有一个人，家中有一妻一妾。那人每天外出，必定吃得饱饱的，喝得醉醺醺地回家。妻子问他和什么人一起吃喝，他说都是一些有钱有势的人。妻便对妾说："丈夫每次外出，一定吃饱喝醉才回来。问他同什么人在一起，他说都是些有钱有势的人，可是从未见有什么显贵的人到我们家来，我想暗中看他究竟去什么地方。"第二天一早，她便尾随丈夫出了家门，发现丈夫走遍城里竟没有一个人和他说句话。最后一直跟到东郊外的坟地，见丈夫向祭扫坟墓的人乞讨些残酒剩饭，没吃饱又东张西望地跑到别处乞讨——这便是他吃饱喝醉的办法。

妻子回到家里，把她看到的情况一五一十告诉了妾又说："丈夫是我们的靠山，想不到他竟是这样……"两个人正在家里边哭边咒骂她们的丈夫。丈夫还不知道怎么回事，这时喜形于色地从外面回来，挺胸叠肚地又向他的妻妾摆威风。

由君子看来，那些不择手段乞求升官发财的人，能够不使他们的妻妾引为羞耻而哭泣的，太少了。

九、万章上篇
Wan Zhang, Part One

《孟子》之第九篇。本篇孟子多谈舜帝之美德。本篇共9章，节选其中3章。

桃应对老师所讲舜的孝道有些不理解，就又问道："您说舜既然如此大孝，那为什么他不告诉父母就娶了尧的两个女儿为妻呢？"孟子就给他们讲舜娶妻不告父母的原因。

9.1 （孟子）曰："人少，则慕父母；知好色，则慕少艾；有妻子，则慕妻子；仕则慕君，不得于君则热中。大孝终身慕父母。"

《万章上篇·1》节选

Mincius said, "One loves his parents when he is young; he wants young and beautiful girls when he learns about love; he loves his wife when he gets married; he seeks to win his sovereign's favor when he becomes an official, indeed he is anxious if he can not. But only the most filial son will love his parents all his life."

孟子说："人小的时候，就知道依恋父母；知道美色时，便想得到年轻漂亮的女子；娶妻之后，便迷恋妻室；做了官，便想讨好君主，得不到君主的欢心，便急得抓耳挠腮。只有最孝顺的人才会终身怀恋父母。"

9.6 （孟子）曰："匹夫而有天下者，德必若舜禹，而又有天子荐之者，故仲尼不有天下。继世以有天下，天之所废，必若桀纣者也，故益、伊尹、周公不有天下。伊尹相汤以王于天下，汤崩，太丁未立，外丙二年，仲壬四年，太甲颠覆汤之典刑，伊尹放之于桐，三年，太甲悔过，自怨自艾，于桐处仁迁义，三年，以听伊尹之训己也，复归于亳。周公之不有天下，犹益之于夏、伊尹之于殷也。"

《万章上篇·6》节选

丹朱：尧之子。**外丙、仲壬**：卜辞作卜丙、中壬。**桐**：地名，故地一说在今河南省偃师县西南。**亳**：地名，故地一说在今河南省偃师县西。

Mencius said, "An ordinary man must be as virtuous as Shun and Yu if he rules over the empire, but he must be recommended by the emperor. So, though Confucius was a saint, he could not rule over the empire because no emperor recommended him to Heaven. Emperors rejected by Heaven end up as tyrannical and wicked as Jie of the Xia Dynasty and Zhou of the Shang Dynasty, though the latter came to the throne by virtue of being the sons of emperors. So Yi, Yiyin and the Duke of Zhou, though virtuous enough, could not rule over the empire because the emperors they served were not as wicked as Jie and Zhou. Yiyin assisted Tang to unify the empire. After Tang's demise, Taiding died before he could succeed to the throne. After two years of rule by Waibing and four years of rule by Zhongren, Taijia, son of Taiding, succeeded to the throne. But he overturned the laws enacted by Tang, so Yiyin exiled him to Tongyi. He repented three years later and was able to be benevolent and righteous in Tongyi. After another three years he was able to act strictly according to the instructions of Yiyin, so he was allowed to return to the capital, Bo, and resume the throne. The Duke of Zhou, just like Yi of the Xia Dynasty and Yiyin of the Yin Dynasty, could not rule the empire."

孟子说:"以一个老百姓而竟得到天下的,他的道德必然像舜和禹一样,而且还要有天子举荐他,所以孔子虽是圣人,因为没有天子的举荐，便不能得到天下。世代相传而得天下的，天所要废弃的，一定是像夏桀、商纣那样残暴无德的，所以，益、伊尹、周公虽然都是道德高尚的贤圣，因所逢君主不像桀、纣，便也不能得到天下。伊尹帮助汤统一了天下，汤死后，太丁未立就死了，外丙在位二年，仲壬在位四年，太丁的儿子太甲又继承王位。太甲破坏了汤的法度，伊尹便把他流放到桐邑，三年之后，太甲悔过，在桐邑能够以仁居心，唯义是从，又过了三年，完全听从伊尹的教诲，然后回到亳都又做了天子。周公不能得到天下，就好像益在夏朝，伊尹在殷朝一样。"

9.9 万章问曰："或曰，'百里奚自鬻于秦养牲者五羊之皮食牛以要秦穆公。'信乎？"孟子曰："否，不然；好事者为之也。百里奚，虞人也。晋人以垂棘之璧与屈产之乘假道于虞以伐虢。宫之奇谏，百里奚不谏。知虞公之不可谏而去之秦，年已七十矣；曾不知以食牛干秦穆公之为污也，可谓智乎？不可谏而不谏，可谓不智乎？知虞公之将亡而先去之，不可谓不智也。时举于秦，知穆公之可与有行也而相之，可谓不智乎？相秦而显其君于天下，可传于后世，不贤而能之乎？自鬻以成其君，乡党自好者不为，而谓贤者为之乎？"

《万章上篇·9》

百里奚：春秋时秦穆公贤相。原为虞大夫。关于他的传说故事（特别是入秦事），古书中颇多异处。**秦穆公**：春秋时秦国君。嬴姓，名任好。春秋五霸之一。**垂棘**：晋国地名，故地所在已不可考，当时以出产玉有名。**屈**：地名，故地所在已不可考，当时以出良马有名。**虞**：国名，周时建立的诸侯国。姬姓。春秋时，为晋所灭。地在今山西省平陆县东北。**虢**：国名，周时建立的诸侯国。姬姓，春秋时，为晋所灭。地在今山西省平陆县。

Wan Zhang asked, "It is said that Baili Xi sold himself to a herdsman in the State of Qin for five sheep skins and tended his cattle, waiting for an appointment from Duke Mu of Qin. Is this reliable?"

Mencius said, "No, it is not. This was fabricated by busybodies. Baili Xi was a minister of the State of Yu. The State of Jin offered fine jade and chariots to Yu, asking for permission to go through Yu to attack the State of Guo. Gong Zhiqi, a minister of Yu, advised the ruler of Yu not to grant Jin's request. But Baili Xi did not give any advice, because he knew that the ruler would not listen. So he left Yu for Qin. At the time he was seventy years of age already. Could he not know that it would be disgraceful to seek an appointment from Duke Mu of Qin by tending cattle? He did not give advice to the ruler of Yu because he knew that the ruler would not listen. Could we say he was not intelligent enough to give advice? He left Yu because he foresaw that Yu would soon be annihilated after its ruler granted Jin's request. We cannot say that he was not wise to do this. He knew that Duke Mu of Qin was a capable ruler worth assisting, and so he assisted Duke Mu of Qin with all his heart when he was recommended. Can we say that his choice was not a wise one? He became a minister of Qin and made Duke Mu of Qin famous throughout the world for generations. Could he have done all this if he had not been a virtuous and wise man? Could a man who, to preserve himself unsullied, would not sell himself to help his sovereign achieve his aims, be called virtuous and wise?"

Notes: Baili Xi: A virtuous prime minister in the reign of Duke Mu of Qin, originally a minister in the State of Yu. There are various accounts of his defection to Qin.

Duke Mu of Qin: One of the five hegemony during the Spring and Autumn Period.

Yu: Name of a state of the Spring and Autumn Period. Its location was in the northeast of present-day Pinglu County, Shanxi Province.

The State of Guo: It was founded in the Zhou Dynasty and annihilated by the State of Jin in the Spring and Autumn Period. Its location was in the present-day Pinglu County, Shanxi Province.

万章问道："有人说，'百里奚以五张羊皮的价钱把自己卖给秦国一个饲养牲畜的人，先替人喂牛，为的是有机会向秦穆公求官。'这话可信吗？"

孟子答道："不，不是这样的。这是好事之徒捏造出来的。百里奚是虞国人。晋国以上等美玉和良马向虞国借道，以使晋军能通过虞国去攻打虢国。当时虞国大臣宫之奇谏阻虞公，劝他不要答应晋国的要求，百里奚却不去劝阻，因为他知道虞公是不会听从劝阻的，于是自己离开虞国，来到秦国，这时他已经七十岁了。他难道不知道以饲养牛来有所求秦穆公是一种不光彩的行为吗？但是，他能够预见虞公不听劝阻，便不去劝阻，这能说他不明智吗？他又能预见到虞国答应晋国的要求后不久将要灭亡，因而早早离开，又不能说他不聪明。当他在秦国被举荐出来时，便知道秦穆公是位可以辅助而有作为的君主，因而倾力辅助他，难道能说他的选择不明智吗？他为秦国卿相，使穆公名显天下，并留名后世，不是贤者能够做得到吗？卖自身而成全君主，一个能够洁身自好的乡下人都不会做的，难道说一个贤者会去做吗？"

十、万章下篇
Wan Zhang, Part Two

《孟子》之第十篇。孟子谈交往,提出"不挟长,不挟贵,不挟兄弟"和"心存恭敬"的原则。本篇共9章,节选其中4章。

孟子对弟子们说:"人皆有不忍人之心。先王有不忍人之心,斯有不忍人之政矣。以不忍人之心,行不忍人之政,治天下可运之掌上。"(《孟子·公孙丑上》)

10.1　孟子曰："伯夷，目不视恶色，耳不听恶声。非其君，不事；非其民，不使。治则进，乱则退。横政之所出，横民之所止，不忍居也。思与乡人处，如以朝衣朝冠坐于涂炭也。当纣之时，居北海之滨，以待天下之清也。故闻伯夷之风者，顽夫廉，懦夫有立志。"

……

孟子曰："伯夷，圣之清者也；伊尹，圣之任者也；柳下惠，圣之和者也；孔子，圣之时者也。孔子之谓集大成。集大成也者，金声而玉振之也。金声也者，始条理也；玉振之也者，终条理也。始条理者，智之事也；终条理者，圣之事也。智，譬则巧也；圣，譬则力也。由射于百步之外也，其至，尔力也；其中，非尔力也。"

《万章下篇·1》节选

　　Mencius said, "Boyi's eyes would not look at what was evil, nor would his ears listen to what was evil. He would not serve anyone but his proper ruler, nor would he rule any but his proper people. He would hold office in time of peace and would retire in time of tumult. He would not reside in any kingdom where a tyrant ruled and the people were lawless. For him, mixing with the common people was like sitting in the dirt wearing court attire. During the reign of King Zhou of the Shang Dynasty, he lived on the shore of the North Sea to wait for improvements in the empire. So anyone who heard about his behavior became honest if he had previously been a corrupt person, and would become strong-willed if he had previously been a coward."
　　……
　　Mencius said, "Boyi was the one sage who was aloof from benefit; Yiyin was the one sage who would always take responsibility; Liuxia Hui was the one sage who could adapt himself to all circumstances. And Confucius was the sage who understood

the times. Confucius can be said to have been the embodiment of all good qualities. By 'embodiment of all good qualities' we mean, using an analogy with music, starting a concert with a bell and terminating it with a chime, so that any job is carried out to its end. The sound of a bell is the commencement of a rhythm, and the sound of a chime is the termination of the rhythm. It is wisdom that starts the rhythm, and it is the sage who puts an end to the rhythm. Wisdom can be likened to skill and the sage to strength. In shooting at a target that is a hundred paces away, it is your strength that causes the arrow to reach it, but it is not strength that causes the arrow to hit it."

孟子说："伯夷，眼不看邪恶的东西，耳不听邪恶的声音。不侍奉不是他理想的君主，不役使不是他理想的百姓。天下太平，就出来做官；天下大乱，便隐退不仕。施行暴政的国家和有暴民居住的地方，他都不去住。他认为和乡下人在一起，就好像穿戴着礼服礼帽而身处肮脏的地方。当商纣王的时候，他住在北海之滨，以待天下清平。所以听到伯夷作风的人，贪得无厌者会变得廉洁，懦弱的人会坚强起来。"

……

孟子又说:"伯夷是圣人中清高的人,伊尹是圣人中负责的人,柳下惠是圣人中随和的人,孔子则是圣人中识时务的人。孔子,可以说是一位集大成者。集大成的意思,犹如作乐先撞钟,以发众声,乐将止时,以磬结束一样有始有终。先撞钟,是节奏的开始;以磬结束,是节奏的终结。节奏开始在于智,节奏终结在于圣。智好比技巧,圣好比力气。犹如射箭,在百步以外能够射到靶子,是你的力量;能够射中靶心,却不仅仅是力量所能做到的了。"

10.3 万章问曰:"敢问友。"孟子曰:"不挟长,不挟贵,不挟兄弟而友。友也者,友其德也,不可以有挟也。"

《万章下篇·3》节选

Wan Zhang said, "May I enquire about the nature of friendship?"

Mencius replied, "The principle is not to take advantage of one's seniority or high position or the high positions of one's relatives. When one befriends others, what he should take into consideration is the others' good qualities and not other things."

万章问道:"请问交朋友的原则。"

孟子答道:"不依仗自己年纪大,不依仗自己地位高,不依仗自己兄弟的富贵。交朋友,是看中朋友的品德而交,心中就不存在有任何依仗的观念。"

10.4 万章问曰:"敢问交际何心也?"孟子曰:"恭也。"曰:"'却之却之为不恭',何哉?"曰:"尊者赐之,曰,'其所取之者义乎,不义乎?'而后受之,以是为不恭,故弗却也。"

《万章下篇·4》节选

Wan Zhang said, "I venture to ask what attitude should one take in communicating with others?"

Mencius said, "A respectful one."

Wang Zhang said, "Why is it said, 'It is disrespectful to refuse another's gift more than once?"

Mencius said, "When a gift is bestowed by a superior, it would be disrespectful for one to accept it only after pondering whether it was ill-gotten or not. So, the gift should not be refused."

万章问道:"请问交际的时候,以何存心?"

孟子答道:"心存恭敬。"

万章说:"为什么说,'一再拒绝别人的礼物,是不恭敬的'?"

孟子说:"尊贵的人有所赐予,如果自己先要想清楚'他这礼物是否不义之财'再决定接受下来,这便是不恭敬,因此,这是不能拒绝的。"

10.5 孟子曰:"仕非为贫也,而有时乎为贫;娶妻非为养也,而有时乎为养。为贫者,辞尊居卑,辞富居贫。辞尊居卑,辞富居贫,恶乎宜乎?抱关击柝。"

《万章下篇·5》节选

Mencius said, "It is not usually because of poverty that a man takes office, but sometimes it is because of poverty. It is not to support one's parents that one takes a wife, but sometimes it is to support one's parents. If one takes office on account of poverty, one should decline a high post and handsome salary, but take a low post and meager emolument. Then what posts would suit his purpose best? The post of a gatekeeper or night watchman would do."

孟子说:"做官不是因为贫穷,但有时候也因为贫穷而做官。娶妻不是为着孝养父母,但有时候也有为着孝养父母而娶妻。因为贫穷而做官的,应该拒绝高官厚禄,居于卑位,只受薄俸。那居于什么位置才合宜呢?就像守门打更的小吏就行了。"

十一、告子上篇
Gao Zi, Part One

《孟子》之第十一篇。孟子讲"性善"、"君子、小人"、"天爵、人爵"。本篇共20章,节选其中15章。

孟子对弟子们说:"从天生资质看,可以使人的本性善良,这就是我给你们讲的人性善。至于有的人性不善良,也不是天生如此。"(《孟子·告子上》)

11.1　告子曰："性犹杞柳也，义犹桮棬也；以人性为仁义，犹以杞柳为桮棬。"孟子曰："子能顺杞柳之性而以为桮棬乎？将戕贼杞柳而后以为桮棬也？如将戕贼杞柳而以为桮棬，则亦将戕贼人以为仁义与？率天下之人而祸仁义者，必子之言夫！"

《告子上篇·1》

杞柳：落叶灌木，枝条柔韧，可编制容器。

Gao Zi said, "Human nature is like the purple willow, and righteousness is like a cup and plate. Making human nature benevolent and righteous is like making cups and plates out of purple willow."

Mencius said, "Can you make a cup and plate without injury to the nature of the purple willow, or is it necessary to injure it? If you have to injure the nature of the purple willow in order to make a cup and plate, do you then have to injure human nature in order to make it benevolent and righteous? Your doctrine will lead the people of the world to harm benevolence and righteousness, it seems to me."

Notes: Purple willow: A deciduous bush with pliable and tough branches. It can be used to make containers.

告子说:"人的本性好比杞柳,仁义好比杯盘。把人的本性化为仁义,就好比用杞柳来制作杯盘。"

孟子说:"您是顺着杞柳的本性来编制杯盘呢,还是毁伤杞柳的本性来制作杯盘呢?如果要先毁伤杞柳的本性然后再制作杯盘,也就是说先毁伤人的本性然后再纳之于仁义吗?率领天下人来损害仁义的,一定是您这种学说吧!"

11.2　告子曰:"性犹湍水也,决诸东方则东流,决诸西方则西流。人性之无分于善不善也,犹水之无分于东西也。"

孟子曰:"水信无分于东西,无分于上下乎?人性之善也,犹水之就下也。人无有不善,水无有不下。今夫水，搏而跃之，可使过颡；激而行之，可使在山。是岂水之性哉？其势则然也。人之可使为不善，其性亦犹是也。"

《告子上篇·2》

Gao Zi said, "Human nature is like running water; it will flow to the east if there is an opening to the east, and it would flow to the west if there is an opening to the west. Human nature is indifferent to good or evil, just as water is indifferent to west and east."

Mencius said, "Water is indifferent as to whether it flows eastward or westward, but is it indifferent as to whether it flows upward or downward? Human nature tends toward good, just as water tends to flow downward. There is no human nature that is not good, and there is no water that does not tend to flow downward. Of course, striking water can make it jump up at one's forehead, and bailing water can make it flow backward or flow toward mountains. But how can such phenomena be attributed to the nature of water? External force is the cause. Man can do evil against nature, like water, can be changed by external force."

告子说:"人性好比急流水,从东边开口便向东流,从西边开口便向西流。人性没有善与不善的定性,就像水没有东流西流的定向一样。"

孟子说:"水固然没有东流西流的定向,难道也没有向上或向下的定向吗?人性本善,就像水向低处流一样。人的本性没有不善良的,水没有不向低处流的。当然,拍打水面使水跳起来,可以高过额头,戽水使水倒流,也可以流于山中。这难道是水的本性吗?形势使它如此的。人可以做坏事,本性的改变也正像水一样。"

11.3 告子曰:"生之谓性。"孟子曰:"生之谓性也,犹白之谓白与?"曰:"然。""白羽之白也,犹白雪之白;白雪之白犹白玉之白与?"曰:"然。""然则犬之性犹牛之性,牛之性犹人之性与?"

《告子上篇·3》

Gao Zi said, "What is inborn is called nature."

Mencius said, "If what is inborn is called nature, then is all that is white called white?"

Gao Zi said, "Yes."

Mencius said, "Is the whiteness of a white feather the same as the whiteness of white snow, and is the whiteness of white snow the same as the whiteness of white jade?"

Gao Zi said, "Yes."

Mencius said, "Then, is the nature of a dog the same as the nature of a cow, and is the nature of a cow the same as the nature of a human being?"

告子说:"天生的资质叫做性。"

孟子说:"天生的资质叫做性,好比一切白的东西都叫白吗?"

告子说:"对。"

孟子说:"白羽毛的白犹如白雪的白,白雪的白犹如白玉的白吗?"

告子说:"对。"

孟子说:"那么,狗性犹如牛性,牛性犹如人性吗?"

11.4 告子曰:"食色,性也。仁,内也,非外也;义,外也,非内也。"孟子曰:"何以谓仁内义外也?"曰:"彼长而我长之,非有长于我也;犹彼白而我白之,从其白于外也,故谓之外也。"曰:"异于白马之白也,无以异于白人之白也;不识长马之长也,无以异于长人之长与?且谓长者义乎?长之者义乎?"曰:"吾弟则爱之,秦人之弟则不爱也,是以我为悦者也,故谓之内。长楚人之长,亦长吾之长,是以长为悦者也,故谓之外也。"曰:"耆秦人之炙,无以异于耆吾炙,夫物则亦有然者也,然则耆炙亦有外与?"

《告子上篇·4》

Gao Zi said, "It is human nature to enjoy food and sex. Benevolence is an internal quality, not an external quality, and righteousness is external, not internal."

Mencius said, "How is it that benevolence is an internal quality and righteousness an external?"

Gao Zi said, "If I give respect to someone simply because of his seniority, the respect is not internal, because my respecting does not come from my heart. It is just like my calling a white thing white because I think it is white. So I say it is an external quality."

Mencius said, "There is probably no difference between the whiteness of a white horse and the whiteness of a white man. But is there also no difference between sympathy shown to an old horse and respect shown to an old man? Now, does the righteousness you mentioned refer to an old man or to the man who respects an old man?"

Gao Zi said, "I love my brother because he is my brother, but I would not love him if he were the brother of a man from Qin. I do so because it is up to me to decide. So I say benevolence is an internal quality. Showing respect both to an old man from Chu and an old man of one's own country is due to the seniority of both. So I say righteousness is an external quality."

Mencius said, "There is no difference between the enjoyment of meat roasted by a man from Qin and that roasted by one's own countryman. Then would you say enjoyment of roasted meat is also an external quality?"

告子说:"饮食男女,这是本性。仁是内在的东西,不是外在的东西;义是外在的东西,不是内在的东西。"

孟子说:"怎样叫做仁是内在的东西,义是外在的东西呢?"

告子说:"因为他年纪大,于是我对他表示恭敬,这恭敬之心不是心中原有的。就好像一个东西是白色的,我就认为它是白色的,这是我对这个白色的东西加以认识的缘故,所以说是外在的东西。"

孟子说:"白马的白和白人的白或者没有什么不一样,但是不知道对一匹老马的怜悯心和对一位长者的恭敬心是不是也没有什么不同呢?而且您说,所谓义,在于老者呢?还是在于恭敬老者的人呢?"

告子说:"因为是我的兄弟便爱他,要是秦国人的兄弟便不爱他,这是因我个人的关系而乐于这样的,所以说仁是内在的东西。恭敬楚国的老人,也恭敬自己的老人,这是因为老人的关系而乐于这样的,所以说义是外在的东西。"

孟子说:"喜欢吃秦国人烧的肉,和喜欢吃自己烧的肉没有什么不一样,那么,难道喜欢吃烧肉的心也是外在的东西吗?"

11.6 孟子曰:"乃若其情,则可以为善矣,乃所谓善也。若夫为不善,非才之罪也。恻隐之心,人皆有之;羞恶之心,人皆有之;恭敬之心,人皆有之;是非之心,人皆有之。恻隐之心,仁也;羞恶之心,义也;恭敬之心,礼也;是非之心,智也。仁义礼智,非由外铄我也。我固有之也,弗思耳矣。故曰,'求则得之,舍则失之。'或相倍蓰而无算者,不能尽其才者也。"

《告子上篇·6》节选

Mencius said, "The inborn quality of human beings can make human nature good. This is what I mean by human nature being good. If someone's nature is not good, it is not because he was born bad. Compassion is common to all; so are the senses of shame, respect, and right and wrong. Compassion gives rise to benevolence, a sense of shame to righteousness, respect to propriety, and sense of right and wrong to wisdom. Benevolence, righteousness, propriety and wisdom are not endowed by others, but are inborn; it is just that one has not reflected upon them. So it is said, 'Seek and you will find it, abandon it and you will lose it.' Some can be twice, five times or countless times better than others because one's nature is inexhaustible."

孟子说:"从天生资质看,可以使人的本性善良,这便是我所说的人性善良。至于有些人性不善良,也不是天生如此。同情心,每个人都有;羞耻心,每个人都有;恭敬心,每个人都有;是非心,每个人都有。同情心属于仁,羞耻心属于义,恭敬心属于礼,是非心属于智。这仁义礼智,不是由外人给予我的,而是我本来就有的，不过不曾认真想罢了。所以说，'探求便会得到，舍弃便会失掉'。人与人之间有相差一倍、五倍甚至无数倍的，就是因为有的人不能充分发挥他们的本性的缘故。"

11.7 孟子曰："富岁，子弟多赖；凶岁，子弟多暴，非天之降才尔殊也，其所以陷溺其心者然也。"

《告子上篇·7》节选

Mencius said, "In good years young men tend to be lazy while in bad years they tend to be violent. But this is not due to difference in their natures; it is due to changes in their natures caused by their environment."

孟子说："丰收年成，少年子弟多半懒惰；灾荒年成，少年子弟多半强暴。这不是天生资质有这样的不同，是由于环境使他们的本性改变的缘故。"

11.8 孟子曰："牛山之木尝美矣，以其郊于大国也。斧斤伐之，可以为美乎？是其日夜之所息，雨露之所润，非无萌蘖之生焉，牛羊又从而牧之，是以若彼濯濯也。人见其濯濯也，以为未尝有材焉，此岂山之性也哉？虽存乎人者，岂无仁义之心哉？其所以放其良心者，亦犹斧斤之于木也，旦旦而伐之，可以为美乎？其日夜之所息，平旦之气，其好恶与人相近也者几希，则其旦昼之所为，有梏亡之矣。梏之反覆，则其夜气不足以存；夜气不足以存，则其违禽兽不远矣。人见其禽兽也，而以为未尝有才焉者，是岂人之情也哉？故苟得其养，无物不长；苟失其养，无物不消。孔子曰：'操则存，舍则亡；出入无时，莫知其乡。'惟心之谓与？"

《告子上篇·8》

牛山：山名。在当时齐国都城临淄南郊。**大国**：谓齐国都城临淄，是当时大都市之一。

Mencius said, "Mount Niu once had fine trees. But as it was located in a suburb of a big city, people frequently cut wood there. How could the fine trees survive? Of course, after being felled, the stumps, with respite for some time and moistened by rain and dew, would put out new buds, but herds of cattle and sheep on the mountain soon ate up all the tender buds, and in the end the mountain became bare. People, seeing the barrenness of the mountain, would think there had never been lush forests on it. Is this barrenness the nature of the mountain? Is there a heart with no benevolence and righteousness? But these are lost just like the trees vanished. Can trees grow if felled day by day? Some people indulge in reflection, with the intention of restoring the good to their hearts. But once they return to society, their newly sprouted intention of restoring the good to their hearts is abandoned. In this respect they are not far from birds and beasts. Other people, seeing their evil behavior as the same as that of birds and beasts, take their nature as bad. But is their nature really bad? With the right nutrition, there is nothing that will not grow under necessary conditions; without it there is nothing that will not perish. Confucius said, 'Hold on to it, and it will remain; let go of it, and it will disappear. It comes and goes, and there is no knowing its direction.' What he was referring to was human hearts."

Notes: Mount Niu: A mountain south of Linzi, capital of the State of Qi. Big city: Linzi.

孟子说:"牛山上的树木曾经是很茂盛的,因为它地处大都市的郊外,经常有人砍伐,它还能够茂盛吗? 当然,砍伐之后由于得到了休息和雨露的滋润,又会发出新芽,但又接着在山上放牧牛羊,很快将嫩芽啃光,久而久之就变成现在这样光秃秃的一座山了。大家看见它那光秃秃的样子,便以为这山上不曾有过茂盛的森林,这难道是山的本来面目吗? 在某些人身上,难道是本来就没有仁义之心吗? 他们之所以丧失了善良之心,也是像砍伐山上的树木一样,每天每时不断地砍伐,树木还能生长吗? 那些人也一样,他们也会本能地有所反思,思想上也会生发出一些恢复善性的萌芽。可是一回到现实中去,就把那刚刚萌生出来的向善的念头淹灭了。时间久了,那向善的念头就会彻底消失了,这个人也就和禽兽的距离越来越近了。别人只看到他的恶行和禽兽一样,就以为这人本性就很坏,这难道是这些人的本性吗?所以说,假如得到必要的条件,万物皆可生长;没有这些必要的条件,任何东西都会消亡。孔子说过,"抓住它,就存在;放弃它,就亡失。出入无时,不知何从。'这是指人心而说的吧。"

11.9 孟子曰:"无或乎王之不智也。虽有天下易生之物也,一日暴之,十日寒之,未有能生者也。吾见亦罕矣,吾退而寒之者至矣,吾如有萌焉何哉?今夫弈之为数,小数也;不专心致志,则不得也。弈秋,通国之善弈者也。使弈秋诲二人弈,其一人专心致志,惟弈秋之为听。一人虽听之,一心以为有鸿鹄将至,思援弓缴而射之,虽与之俱学，弗若之矣。为是其智弗若兴？曰：非然也。"

《告子上篇·9》

奕秋：古代棋圣。

Mencius said, "It is no surprise that the king lacks wisdom. Even a plant that grows readily will not be able to grow if it is exposed to the sun for one day and to the bitter cold for ten days. I have seldom called on the king since I retired and exposed him to the cold. Even though he held good intentions, I did not help him. Take chess-playing, for example. Though chess-playing is a petty skill, if one cannot devote his heart to it, he will not be able to master the skill. Yiqiu was a master of chess-playing. If he was asked to instruct two persons to play chess and if one devoted all his heart to it and the other, though listening to the instruction, was thinking of something else and was absent-minded, it would be certain he would not be able to attain the same achievement as the other though they attended the same class. Would it be because he was less intelligent than the other? Obviously not."

Note: Yiqiu: An ancient master chess player.

孟子说:"王的不聪明是不足为怪的。就是一种最易成活的植物,如果对它晒一天,冻十天,它也是长不好的。我退居以后,和王很少相见,使他冷落,他虽有向善的念头,我却没有帮助它生长。譬如下围棋,这虽不过是小技艺而已,如果不能专心致志,也是学不好的。奕秋是全国的棋圣。假如让他同时教两个人,一个人专心致志,认真领会老师的讲解。另一个人虽也在听讲,而脑子里却在想入非非,心不在焉。这样,虽然他和人家一道学习,成绩肯定不如人家。这是因为他不如人家聪明吗?显然不是的。"

11.10 孟子曰:"鱼,我所欲也,熊掌亦我所欲也;二者不可得兼,舍鱼而取熊掌者也。生亦我所欲也,义亦我所欲也;二者不可得兼,舍生而取义者也。生亦我所欲,所欲有甚于生者,故不为苟得也。""一箪食,一豆羹,得之则生,弗得则死,呼尔而与之,行道之人弗受;蹴尔而与之,乞人不屑也。"

《告子上篇·10》节选

Mencius said, "Fish is what I want and bear's paw* is also what I want. If I cannot have both, I prefer bear's paw to fish. Life is what I treasure and righteousness is also what I treasure. If I cannot have both, I prefer righteousness to life. Though life is what I treasure, there is something that is more precious to me, and that is righteousness. So I will not draw on an ignoble existence." " When one is in extreme poverty, a bowl of rice and a bowl of soup will keep one alive; without them, one will starve to death. But if these things are given to him in contempt, even a hungry man will not take them. If alms are given like food to dogs and horses, even a beggar will not tolerate the contempt."

Note: * A delicacy in ancient China.

孟子说:"鱼是我喜欢吃的,熊掌也是我喜欢吃的,如果两者不能同时得到,我便会舍鱼而要熊掌。生命是我所宝贵的,义也是我所宝贵的。如果两者发生矛盾,必须舍弃一种时,我便会牺牲生命,而取义。生命虽然是我所宝贵的,但对我来说还有比生命更为宝贵的,那就是义。所以我不做苟且偷生的事。""人在穷困的时候,一碗饭,一碗汤,得到它便能活下去,得不到它便会饿死,但如果是嗟来之食,就是饿人也不会去吃的,如果像对待狗马那样的施舍就是乞丐也不屑于接受这种侮辱。"

11.11 孟子曰:"仁,人心也;义,人路也。舍其路而弗由,放其心而不知求,哀哉!人有鸡犬放,则知求之;有放心而不知求。学问之道无他,求其放心而已矣。"

《告子上篇·11》

Mencius said, "Benevolence is the heart of a man, righteousness the road. How sad it is one should depart from the right road and not seek the heart that has gone astray, alas! When a dog or chicken is lost, people search for them, but not for a heart that is lost. Learning is nothing but seeking the lost heart."

孟子说:"仁是人的心,义是人的路。放弃正路而不走,丧失了善良之心不知寻找,可悲呀!家里的鸡或狗丢了还知道去找,而心丢了却反而不知道去找。学问之道没有别的,就是把丧失的良心找回来罢了。"

11.12 孟子曰:"今有无名之指屈而不信,非疾痛害事也,如有能信之者,则不远秦楚之路,为指之不若人也。指不若人,则知恶之;心不若人,则不知恶,此之谓不知类也。"

《告子上篇·12》

Mencius said, "A man, one of whose fingers is bent and cannot be straightened, would go all the way from Qin to Chu to have his finger cured if he knew that there were someone able to straighten it, though the bent finger hurt him not, nor did it hamper his business. It would be simply because one of his fingers was not as good as others'. He hates it when his finger is not as good as others', but he knows not how to resent it when his heart is not as good as others'. This is called ignorance of the relative importance of things."

孟子说:"现在有人一个手指伸不直,虽然不痛苦,也不妨碍工作,却到处求治,如果听说有人能使它伸直,就是秦国、楚国也不以路远,一定去医治,就因为自己的一个手指头不如别人。一个手指不如别人,就知道厌恶,心性(仁)不及别人,却不知道厌恶,这叫做不知道轻重。"

11.13 孟子曰:"拱把之桐梓,人苟欲生之,皆知所以养之者。至于身,而不知所以养之者,岂爱身不若桐梓哉?弗思甚也。"

《告子上篇·13》

Mencius said,"Everyone knows how to tend a tung tree or Chinese catalpa. But he does not know how to cultivate himself. Is care for a tree more important than care for oneself? This is want of reflection in the extreme."

孟子说:"一两把粗的桐树梓树,若要使它成材,都晓得如何去培养。至于本人,却不知道如何去培养自己成材,难道爱自己还不及爱树木吗?真是太不知道动脑筋了。"

11.15 公都子问曰:"钧是人也,或为大人,或为小人,何也?"孟子曰:"从其大体为大人,从其小体为小人。"曰:"钧是人也,或从其大体,或从其小体,何也?"曰:"耳目之官不思,而蔽于物。物交物,则引之而已矣。心之官则思,思则得之,不思则不得也。此天之所与我者。先立乎其大者,则其小者不能夺也。此为大人而已矣。"

《告子上篇·15》

Gong Duzi asked, "Since all are equally men, why are some gentlemen and some petty men?"

Mencius said, "Those who aspire to satisfy the needs of the important parts of their bodies are gentlemen, and those who aspire to satisfy the needs of the less-important parts of their bodies are petty men."

Gong Duzi asked, "Since all are equally men, why do some aspire to satisfy the needs of the important parts of their bodies and others the needs of the less-important parts of their bodies?"

Mencius said, "Organs such as the ear and the eye are incapable of thought, and so are easily deceived by external things; they are led astray once they come into contact with external things. The heart, however, specializes in contemplation. The good nature of a man can only be attained after contemplation; otherwise it will be lost. This organ is bestowed upon human beings by Heaven, so it is an important organ. Once the status of the important organ is established, the less-important organs will not be able to change the man's nature, and the man will be a gentleman."

公都子问道:"同样是人,为什么有君子,有小人?"

孟子说:"求满足身体重要器官的需要的是君子,求满足身体次要器官的欲望的是小人。"

公都子问:"同样是人,为什么有人要求满足重要器官的需要,有人要求满足次要器官的需要?"

孟子说:"耳朵眼睛这类器官不会思考,故会被外物所蒙蔽。一接触外物,便会被引向迷途了。心这个器官专职思考,人的善性,思考便得之,不思考便失之。这个器官是天特意给我们人类的。因此,这是重要器官,要先把它树立起来,那么,次要器官便不能移其性了。于是便成了君子。"

11.16 孟子曰:"有天爵者,有人爵者。仁义忠信,乐善不倦,此天爵也;公卿大夫,此人爵也。古之人修其天爵,而人爵从之。今之人修其天爵,以要人爵;既得人爵,而弃其天爵,则惑之甚者也,终亦必亡而已矣。"

《告子上篇·16》

天爵、人爵：古代称不居官位，因德高而受人尊敬者，如受天然的爵位。与此对称，在朝为官者为人爵。爵，爵位：君主国家贵族封号的等级。

Mencius said, "There is nobility in nature and nobility in society. Benevolence, righteousness, loyalty, faithfulness and unwearied joy in what is good are nobility in nature. Dukes, ministers and high officials are nobility in society. The people of old strove to reach nobility in nature, and nobility in society followed naturally. People today strive to reach nobility in nature only to attain nobility in society. Once the latter is attained they discard nobility in nature. This is folly indeed! They are sure to come to a bad end."

Note: Nobility in nature and in society: In ancient times, when a man did not hold a high position in society but was respected by the people for his virtues, he was looked upon as being ennobled by nature. Anyone who held a post at court was one of the social nobility.

孟子说:"有自然爵位,有社会爵位。仁义忠信,好善不倦,这是自然爵位;公卿大夫,是社会爵位。古代人修养他的自然爵位,于是社会爵位随着来了。现代人修养他的自然爵位是用来追求社会爵位,一旦得到社会爵位,便会放弃他的自然爵位,那就太糊涂了,结果连社会爵位也会丧失的。"

11.18 孟子曰:"仁之胜不仁也,犹水胜火。今之为仁者,犹以一杯水救一车薪之火也;不熄,则谓之水不胜火,此又与于不仁之甚者也,亦终必亡而已矣。"

《告子上篇·18》

Mencius said, "Benevolence can overcome cruelty, as water can extinguish fire. These days, those who claim to practice benevolence can be compared to a man who tries to put out a burning cartload of wood with a cup of water. When the fire is not extinguished, he says water cannot quench fire. He no longer believes that benevolence can overcome cruelty. Then he throws in his lot with the unrighteous, and in the end is ruined."

孟子说:"仁胜过不仁,正像水可以灭火一样。今天所谓行仁的人,好像用一杯水来扑灭一车柴的大火,火不能灭,便说水不能灭火,也就不再相信仁胜过不仁的道理。于是这些人又和不仁的人走在了一起,结果连他们已行的一点仁也消失了。"

11. 19 孟子曰:"五谷者,种之美者也;苟为不熟,不如荑稗。夫仁,亦在乎熟之而已矣。"

《告子上篇·19》

荑稗: 两种草名。荑即稊,和稗一样,都是杂草,结实甚小,但可作家畜饲料,古人也用以备凶年。

Mencius said, "The five kinds of grain are the best species of crops. But they are no more useful than weeds if they are not properly ripe. The value of benevolence lies in its capability to make men's benevolence ripen."

孟子说:"五谷虽然是庄稼中的好品种,假若不能成熟,反而不及稊稗有用。仁的好处也在于成为仁人。"

11.20 孟子曰:"羿之教人射,必志于彀;学者亦必志于彀。大匠诲人必以规矩,学者亦必以规矩。"

《告子上篇·20》

孟子这里说的"必志于彀",是防止半途而废的意思;"必以规矩",是防止创述异端邪说的意思。

Mencius said, "Yi, in teaching archery, stressed drawing the bow to its full, and his students followed suit. Great carpenters, when teaching their craft, used compasses and squares, and their students followed suit."

Note: "Drawing the bow to its full" means not giving up halfway; "used compasses and squares" means avoidance of unorthodox opinions.

孟子说:"羿教人射箭,一定拉满弓;学习的人也一定要拉满弓。好的木匠教徒弟,一定依循规矩;学习的人也一定要依循规矩。"

◎ 告子上篇 *Gao Zi, Part One*

十二、告子下篇
Gao Zi, Part Two

《孟子》之第十二篇。孟子提出"五霸者,三王之罪人也。"以此得罪于齐威王的大臣们。本篇共16章,节选其中6章。

魏国人白圭,名丹字圭,曾为魏相,是梁惠王心腹重臣。他嫉妒梁惠王频频接近孟子,听说孟子主张'十分抽一'的税制就故意说:"我想定'二十抽一'的税率,你看怎么样?"孟子说他的所谓"二十抽一"不过是"大桀小桀"罢了。

12.8 鲁欲使慎子为将军。孟子曰:"不教民而用之,谓之殃民。殃民者,不容于尧舜之世。一战胜齐,遂有南阳,然且不可——"

《告子下篇·8》节选

南阳:即汶阳,在泰山之西南,汶水之北。春秋时为齐鲁所争之地。

The State of Lu wanted to make Shen Zi commander of its army. Mencius said, "To ask people to fight without training is to harm the people. Those who harmed the people were not tolerated in the days of Yao and Shun. This should not be tolerated even if Shen Zi can defeat the State of Qi in a single battle and occupy Nanyang."

鲁国打算让慎子作将军。孟子说:"不经训练便让百姓去打仗,这就是陷害百姓。对加害百姓的人,在尧舜时代是不能重用的。即使他能一战而打败齐国,夺取南阳,也是不能重用的。"

12.11 白圭曰:"丹之治水也愈于禹。"孟子曰:"子过矣。禹之治水,水之道也,是故禹以四海为壑。今吾子以邻国为壑。水逆行谓之洚水——洚水者,洪水也——仁人之所恶也。吾子过矣。"

《告子下篇·11》

Baigui said, "I can drain floodwaters better than Yu." Mencius said, "You are wrong. When Yu drained floodwaters, he let the water run its course naturally, so he let the four seas receive the water. But you channeled the water to a neighboring state and caused flooding there. No benevolent man would do that."

白圭说:"我治理水患比大禹还强。"
孟子说:"你错了。禹治理水患,是顺应水的本性而行的,所以禹使水流注于四海。如今你却使水流入邻国。把水患转嫁给邻国,这是仁人所不为的。"

12.12 孟子曰："君子不亮，恶乎执？"

《告子下篇·12》

Mencius said, "How can a gentleman have friends if he is not honest and does not keep his word?"

孟子说："君子不讲诚信，如何能有朋友？"

12.14 陈子曰："古之君子何如则仕？"孟子曰："所就三，所去三。迎之致敬以有礼；言，将行其言也，则就之。礼貌未衰，言弗行也，则去之。其次，虽未行其言也，迎之致敬以有礼，则就之。礼貌衰，则去之。其下，朝不食，夕不食，饥饿不能出门户，君闻之，曰，'吾大者不能行其道，又不能从其言也，使饥饿于我土地，吾耻之。'周之，亦可受也，免死而已矣。"

《告子下篇·14》

陈子：人名。一说即孟子弟子陈臻。

Chen Zi said, "Under what conditions would a gentleman in ancient times assume office?"

Mencius said, "Under three conditions he would assume office, and under three conditions he would leave office. First, if his ruler received him respectfully according to the proper rite and put his advice into practice, he would assume office. But if his advice were not put into practice, he could leave even if he were still treated respectfully. Second, he might still take office if his ruler received him sincerely and earnestly, even if his advice were not put into practice. But he would leave if the ruler snubbed him. Third, if he was so weak from hunger that he could not talk and if his ruler said, 'I cannot practice your ideas, nor can I take your advice, but I am ashamed of letting you starve to death in my state,' and gave him charity, in such circumstances he could also accept an official post, just to ward off starvation."

Note:Chen Zi: Personal name, also said to be Chen Zhen, a disciple of Mencius.

陈子说:"古代的君子在什么情况下才肯出来做官?"

孟子说:"有三种情况下可以就职,有三种情况下可以离职。君主按礼恭敬地迎接,他有所主张,君主又打算实行他的主张,便可就职。虽然对他依然恭敬有礼,但已不再实行他的主张了,便可离职。其次,虽然没有实行他的主张,但君主是诚心地迎接他,也可以就职。一旦君主冷落,便可离职。还有最下一等的,饿得已走不动路了,为了吃饭,君主说,'我不能实行他的主张,又不能听从他的言论,但我不忍让他在我这里挨饿。'于是周济他,这种情况下也可以接受职务,这只是免于饿死罢了。"

12.15 孟子曰:"舜发于畎亩之中,傅说举于版筑之间,胶鬲举于鱼盐之中,管夷吾举于士,孙叔敖举于海,百里奚举于市。故天将降大任于是人也,必先苦其心志,劳其筋骨,饿其体肤,空乏其身,行拂乱其所为,所以动心忍性,曾益其所不能。人恒过,然后能改;困于心,衡于虑,而后作;征于色,发于声,而后喻。入则无法家拂士,出则无敌国外患者,国恒亡。然后知生于忧患而死于安乐也。"

《告子下篇·15》

傅说:殷相。相传说(yuè)曾筑于傅岩之野,武丁访得,举以为相,出现殷中兴局面。**胶鬲**:纣王之臣。**管夷吾**:即管仲。**孙叔敖**:楚国宰相。

Mencius said, "Shun rose from farms; Fuyue was raised to office from among builders; Jiaoge from fish and salt markets; Guan Yiwu was once a prisoner; Sunshu Ao came from a family of low status; and Baili Xi was once sold as slave. This all goes to show that when Heaven intends to bestow a great mission on a person, it makes him suffer in mind and body. It makes him endure starvation, and subjects him to poverty, difficulties and all kinds of tests so as to harden his will power, toughen his nature and increase his capabilities. One can only correct one's mistakes by constantly making mistakes; one can only be stimulated and become creative if one has been frustrated in mind and perplexed in thought and deliberation. He can only be understood if he expresses himself by his countenance and in his speech. A state has no chance of surviving if there are no strict, law-enforcing ministers and scholars capable of offering good advice in court and no constant threats of foreign aggression to guard against. And so we can conclude from this that worry and trouble enable one to survive, while complacency and pleasure will bring about one's downfall."

Notes: Fuyue: Prime minister of Yin. Legend has it that Yue had been a slave laborer in the wilds of Fuyan. Wuding raised him to the post of prime minister, and Yin experienced a revival.

Jiaoge: A minister of the Zhou emperor.

Guanyiwu: Guan Zhong.

Sunshu Ao: Prime minister of the State of Chu.

孟子说:"舜由农夫中兴起,傅说出于苦役之中,胶鬲从鱼盐贱役中被提举出来,管仲曾为囚徒,孙叔敖出身鄙贱,百里奚曾被买卖。所以,天将要把重大使命赋于某人时,必先苦其心志,劳其筋骨,饿其体肤,使他穷困让他历经磨炼,这样,便可以坚强他的心,坚韧他的性情,增长他的能力。一个人经常发生错误,才能改正错误;困苦于心,思虑阻塞,才能有所发愤有所创造;表现在脸上、言语中,才能被人了解。一个国家,国内没有执法严厉的大臣和足以辅弼的士人,国外没有相与抗衡的邻国和外患的忧虑,反倒容易灭亡。这样,就可以知道忧虑患难足以使人生存,安逸快乐足以使人灭亡的道理了。"

12.16 孟子曰:"教亦多术矣,予不屑之教诲也者,是亦教诲之而已矣。"

《告子下篇·16》

Mencius said, "There are many ways of teaching. To neglect purposely to teach is also a way of teaching."

孟子说:"教育有很多种方法,我故意冷落他,促使他发愤,这也是一种教诲的方法。"

十三、尽心上篇
Jin Xin, Part One

《孟子》之第十三篇。"使善良的本心达到极限"即"尽心"也。本篇共46章,节选其中27章。

公元前316年,这一年燕国发生内乱,有人劝齐宣王出兵伐燕,但也有人反对他吞并燕国。齐宣王举棋不定,问孟子可不可以出兵。

13.1 孟子曰:"尽其心者,知其性也。知其性,则知天矣。存其心,养其性,所以事天也。殀寿不贰,修身以俟之,所以立命也。"

《尽心上篇·1》

Mencius said, "To exert one's kind heart to its full is to know one's nature. To know one's nature is to know the will of Heaven. To keep one's own heart and cultivate one's nature are ways to serve Heaven. To cultivate one's body and mind single-mindedly without regard to the length of one's life and wait for whatever might come is the way to settle down with fate."

孟子说:"使善良的本心达到极限,就是懂得了人的本性。懂得了人的本性,就懂得了天命。保持人的本心,培养人的本性,这就是对待天命的方法。短命也好,长寿也好,都不三心二意,只是培养身心,等待天命,这就是安身立命的方法。"

13.3 孟子曰:"求则得之,

舍则失之，是求有益于得也，求在我者也。求之有道，得之有命，是求无益于得也，求在外者也。"

《尽心上篇·3》

Mencius said, "There are things which one can get if one seeks them, and things that one will lose if one slackens one's grip on them. In this case seeking is relevant to obtaining, because what one seeks is in oneself. There are things which one must seek in a certain way, but it is up to fate whether one can get them or not. In this case seeking is irrelevant to obtaining, because what one seeks is outside oneself."

孟子说："有些东西求便会得到，放弃便会失掉，求对于得到是有益的，因为所求的对象在我自身。求有一定的方式，能否得到却听从命运，这求对于得到便是无益的，因为所求的对象在我之外。"

13.4　孟子曰："万物皆备于我矣。反身而诚，乐莫大焉。强恕而行，求仁莫近焉。"

《尽心上篇·4》

Mencius said, "All things are in me. There can be no greater pleasure than to find, after reflection, oneself sincere. Persisting in treating others in the way one wishes to be treated is the shortest way to benevolence."

孟子说："一切我都具备了。反躬自问，自己是真诚的，便是最大的快乐。坚持推己及人的恕道，这是达到仁德的捷径。"

13.5　孟子曰："行之而不著焉，习矣而不察焉，终身由之而不知其道者，众也。"

《尽心上篇·5》

Mencius said, "The common herd acts without understanding the reason for doing so, performs tasks blindly and mechanically, and follows the lifelong road without comprehending its nature."

孟子说："只知去做，却不明白其理，习以为常却不知其所以然。一般人在这条路上走了一辈子，却不明白是条什么路。"

13.6 孟子曰："人不可以无耻，无耻之耻，无耻矣。"

《尽心上篇·6》

Mencius said, "Men should not be without a sense of shame. The shame of not knowing shame is indeed shameless."

孟子说："人不可以没有羞耻之心，不知羞耻的那种羞耻，是真的不知羞耻。"

13.7 孟子曰："耻之于人大矣，为机变之巧者，无所用耻焉。不耻不若人，何若人有？"

《尽心上篇·7》

Mencius said, "A sense of shame is of great importance to men. Cunning and crafty men have no sense of shame. If one has no sense of shame, how can one be considered a proper man?"

孟子说:"羞耻对于人关系重大,机谋巧诈之人是不知道羞耻的。不以落后为耻,怎么能赶上别人呢?"

13.9 (孟子)曰:"尊德乐义,则可以嚣嚣矣。故士穷不失义,达不离道。穷不失义,故士得己焉;达不离道,故民不失望焉。古之人,得志,泽加于民;不得志,修身见于世。穷则独善其身,达则兼善天下。"

《尽心上篇·9》节选

Mencius said, "Value virtue and righteousness, and you will derive pleasure from it. So scholars will not drop righteousness in adversity, nor will they diverge from their principles in times of success. They will not drop righteousness, so they can derive pleasure from it. They will not diverge from their principles, so ordinary people will not be disappointed in them. The ancients would bestow favor on all people when in power, and they would cultivate their own characters when in retirement. In obscurity, they would maintain their own integrity. In times of success, they would make perfect the whole empire."

孟子说:"重德好义,就可以做到自得其乐了。所以,士人穷困时不失义,得意时不离道。穷不失义,所以能自得其乐;得意时不离道,老百姓就不会失望。古代之人,得意,惠泽普施于百姓;失意,修养个人品德。以此种态度处世就能做到失意则独善其身,得意则兼善天下。"

13.10 孟子曰:"待文王而后兴者,凡民也。若夫豪杰之士,虽无文王犹兴。"

《尽心上篇·10》

Mencius said, "Ordinary people are inspired only when a sage king like King Wen emerges. But outstanding people are inspired even without a sage king like King Wen."

孟子说:"一般人一定要等圣王出世而后奋发,至于杰出人才,纵使没有圣王出世也能奋发起来。"

13.12 孟子曰:"以佚道使民,虽劳不怨。以生道杀民,虽死不怨杀者。"

《尽心上篇·12》

Mencius said, "If people are employed in order to ease their lot, they will not begrudge it even if they are driven hard. If people are killed for the sake of saving others' lives, even those who are killed will not begrudge those who kill them."

孟子说:"为了老百姓的安乐而役使百姓,百姓虽劳苦而无怨。为了老百姓的生命安全而杀死坏人,被杀者也不会怨恨杀他的人。"

13.14 孟子曰:"仁言不如仁声之入人深也,善政不如善教之得民也。善政,民畏之;善教,民爱之。善政得民财，善教得民心。"

《尽心上篇·14》

Mencius said, "Benevolent words do not strike root in the heart of people as much as benevolent music does. Good government does not win the hearts of the people as much as good education does. People fear good government, but they love good education. Good government can obtain the wealth created by the people, but good education can win the hearts of the people."

孟子说："仁德的话不如仁德的音乐深入人心，良好的政治不如良好的教育容易获得民心。良好的政治，百姓畏惧它；良好的教育，百姓爱它。良好的政治能得到百姓创造的财富，良好的教育能得到百姓的心。"

13.15 孟子曰："人之所不学而能者，其良能也；所不虑而知者，其良知也。孩提之童无不知爱其亲者，及其长也，无不知敬其兄也。亲亲，仁也；敬长，义也；无他，达之天下也。"

《尽心上篇·15》

Mencius said, "What men can do without learning is a result of inborn ability; what men know without contemplating is a result of intuition. No child does not love his parents, and no child, after he grows up, does not respect his elder brother. To love one's parents is benevolence and to respect one's elder brother is righteousness. Only these two virtues, benevolence and righteousness, are universal virtues."

孟子说："人不待学习便能做到的，这是本能；不待思考便知道的，这是先知。小孩没有不爱他父母的，等他长大，没有不知道恭敬兄长的。爱亲为仁，敬长为义，只有仁和义是通达天下的两种品德。"

13. 16 孟子曰："舜之居深山之中，与木石居，与鹿豕游，其所以异于深山之野人者几希；及其闻一善言，见一善行，若决江河，沛然莫之能御也。"

《尽心上篇·16》

Mencius said, "When Shun lived deep in the mountains, he lived among rocks and sported with deer and boars. There was little difference between him and the rustics of the mountains. But when he heard good words or saw good deeds, he would adopt and follow them, like a river bursting its banks in an unstoppable flood."

孟子说："舜住在山林中时，居则见树木和石头，出门则见鹿和猪，跟山林中的一般人没有什么不同。等他听到一句善言，看到一件善行便立即采纳实行，这种力量像决口的江河一样没有人能阻挡得了。"

13.17 孟子曰："无为其所不为，无欲其所不欲，如此而已矣。"

《尽心上篇·17》

Mencius said, "Do not do what you should not do, and do not desire what you should not desire. That is all."

孟子说:"不干不应干的事,不要不应要的东西,这样就行了。"

13.18 孟子曰:"人之有德慧术知者,恒存乎疢疾。独孤臣孽子,其操心也危,其虑患也深,故达。"

《尽心上篇·18》

Mencius said, "Men acquire virtue, wisdom, capability and talent in adversity. Only estranged ministers and sons born by concubines know all, because they are in a state of constant caution and great worry."

孟子说:"人之所以有道德、聪明、本领、才能,常常存在于忧患之中。只有那些孤臣孽子,他们由于谨言慎行,忧虑深刻,所以能通达事理。"

13.20 孟子曰:"君子有三乐,而王天下不与存焉。父母俱存,兄弟无故,一乐也;仰不愧于天,俯不怍于人,二乐也;得天下英才而教育之,三乐也。君子有三乐,而王天下不与存焉。"

《尽心上篇·20》

Mencius said, "A gentleman delights in three things, but to rule the world is not among these. The first delight is that his parents are hale and hearty and his brothers are safe and well. The second delight is that he feels no shame as he faces Heaven above and the people here below. The third delight is that he can gather together all the talented people in the world and instruct them. A gentleman delights in three things, but to rule the world is not among these."

孟子说:"君子有三种乐事,但不包括以德服天下者。父母健康,兄弟平安,是第一种快乐;上无愧于天,下无愧于人,是第二种快乐;

得天下英才而教育之,是第三种快乐。君子有三种快乐,但不包括以德服天下者。"

13.24 孟子曰:"孔子登东山而小鲁,登泰山而小天下,故观于海者难为水,游于圣人之门者难为言。观水有术,必观其澜。日月有明,容光必照焉。流水之为物也,不盈科不行;君子之志于道也,不成章不达。"

《尽心上篇·24》

东山:一说即蒙山,在今山东省蒙阴县南。

Mencius said, "When Confucius ascended the Eastern Mountain, he realized how small the State of Lu was. When he ascended Mount Tai, he saw how small the empire was. Anyone who has seen the sea will not be impressed by other waters. Anyone who has learned from a sage will not be attracted by other doctrines. There is a way to watch water, that is, to watch its roaring waves. The light of the sun and moon can shine into every corner. Flowing water will pursue its journey only when it has filled all low lying lands. Gentlemen, in their pursuit of principles, will not reach enlightenment without making some achievements first."

Note: Eastern Mountain: Said to be Mount Meng, in the south of Mengyin County, Shandong Province.

孟子说:"孔子登上东山往下看,便觉得鲁国小了。登上泰山,便觉得天下也小了。所以对见过大海的人,别的水就难于吸引他了。对于曾在圣人之门学习过的人,别的学说也就难于吸引他了。看水有个方法,一定要看它壮阔的波涛。日月的光辉能照遍每个角落。流水一定把洼地注满才肯再向前流,君子有志于道,不取得一定的成就,也就不能通达。"

13.26 孟子曰:"杨子取为我,拔一毛而利天下,不为也。墨子兼爱,摩顶放踵利天下,为之。子莫执中。执中为近之。执中无权,犹执一也。所恶执一者,为其贼道也，举一而废百也。"

《尽心上篇·26》

子莫：鲁国之贤人。

Mencius said, "Yangzi put the self first; he would not pluck out a single one of his hairs even if it would benefit the whole world. Mozi favored love without discrimination. He would have suffered hurt from his head to his heels if it could benefit the whole world. Zimo chose the middle way. But to adhere to the middle way without being flexible is being stubbornly biased. Why should I detest stubborn bias? Because it hurts the way of benevolence and righteousness. It sticks to one point without taking other points into account."

Note: Zimo, A worthy of the State of Lu.

孟子说："杨子主张为我，拔一根汗毛而有利于天下也不干。墨子主张兼爱，只要对天下有利，摩顶放踵的事也肯干。子莫主张中庸之道。主张中庸之道就差不多了。但主张中庸如果不知变通，便是偏执。为什么厌恶偏执呢？

因为它损害仁义之道，只是执其一点而不顾其余。"

13.28 孟子曰："柳下惠不以三公易其介。"

《尽心上篇·28》

Mencius said, "Liuxia Hui would not compromise his personal integrity for high office."

孟子说："柳下惠不因为可做高官而改变其操守。"

13.29 孟子曰："有为者辟若掘井，掘井九轫而不及泉，犹为弃井也。"

《尽心上篇·29》

轫：同仞，古代七尺（一说八尺）为一仞。

Mencius said, "Trying to achieve something is like digging a well—even if it is dug down 60 or 70 (Chinese) feet but fails to reach the spring, it is no better than an abandoned well."

孟子说:"做事就像挖井一样,尽管挖了六七丈深,不见泉水仍然是一口废井。"

13.30 孟子曰:"尧舜,性之也;汤武,身之也;五霸,假之也。久假而不归,恶知其非有也。"

《尽心上篇·30》

Mencius said, "Yao and Shun were benevolent and righteous by nature. Tang of the Shang Dynasty and King Wu of the Zhou Dynasty were benevolent and righteous in practice. The five hegemonies seek profit in the name of practicing these virtues. But how do you know that they do not turn their pretense into reality if they keep practicing these deceptions long enough and do not abandon them?"

孟子说:"尧舜实行仁义,是由于本性,因其自然。商汤和周武王实行仁义,是身体力行。春秋五霸不过是假借实行仁义而谋利。但是,借得久了，总不放弃，你又怎能知道他不终于弄假成真了呢。"

13.34 孟子曰："仲子，不义与之齐国而弗受，人皆信之，是舍箪食豆羹之义也。人莫大焉亡亲戚君臣上下。以其小者信其大者，奚可哉？"

《尽心上篇·34》

孟子这里说"仲子，不义与之齐国而弗受"是设想之辞，不是真有其事。相反，仲子避兄离母耻其兄为齐卿（事见《滕文公下》第10章），孟子大不以为然，说他无亲戚君臣上下。是只有小义而无大义。

Mencius said, "All trusted Chen Zhongzi because he declared he would decline to accept the whole State of Qi if it was unrighteous to do so. But this is only petty righteousness, the sort which refuses to accept a bowl of porridge or rice. No crime is more serious than to disown one's parents and brothers and to disregard the relations between sovereign and minister, superior and inferior. But

Chen Zhongzi is just such a man. How can one believe that he would be righteous in major issues on the basis of him being righteous in minor ones?"

Note: Mencius is simply supposing that Chen Zhongzi would refuse to accept the State of Qi. It is not a fact that it was offered to him. Instead, Zhongzi left his elder brother and mother because he felt shame that his elder brother was a minister of Qi. (See the tenth paragraph of "Duke Wen of Teng"). Mencius censured him for disowning his kin, disregarding the relations between sovereign and minister, and superior and inferior, and maintaining righteousness on minor issues only, but not on major ones.

孟子说:"陈仲子,假定把整个齐国交给他,如果不合义,他也不会接受,因此别人都相信他。其实他那种义不过是舍弃一粥一饭的小义。人的罪过没有比不要父兄君臣上下还大的,而仲子便是这种人,因为他有小义,而相信他有大义,这怎么可以呢?"

13.37 孟子曰:"食而弗爱,豕交之也;爱而不敬,兽畜之也。恭敬者,币之未将者也。恭敬而无宾，君子不可虚拘。"

《尽心上篇·37》

Mencius said, "To feed a person without love is to treat him like a hog. To love a person without respect is to treat him like a dog or a horse. Respect should come before feeding. A gentleman cannot be retained by presenting him with gifts but not treating him with respect."

孟子说："对于人只能供给吃喝而并不爱他，等于养猪。爱而不敬，等于畜养狗马。恭敬之心是在供养之前就有的。只是致送礼物，而无恭敬之心，君子不会被这虚套留住。"

13.38 孟子曰："形色，天性也；惟圣人然后可以践形。"

《尽心上篇·38》

Mencius said, "Bodily form and appearance are endowed by Heaven. Outer beauty must be enriched by inner beauty, but this can only be done by a sage."

孟子说："人的身体容貌是天生的,这种外在的美要靠内在的美来充实它,只有圣人才能做到这一点。"

13.40 孟子曰："君子之所以教者五:有如时雨化之者,有成德者,有达财者,有答问者,有私淑艾者。此五者,君子之所以教也。"

《尽心上篇·40》

Mencius said. "There are, for a gentleman, five ways of teaching: by influencing like moistening with rain and dew, by promoting virtue, by cultivating talent, by answering inquiries, and by encouraging self-cultivation. These are the five ways of teaching."

孟子说："君子的教育方法有五种:有像雨露滋润万物的,有促成人品德的,有培养人才能的,有解答疑问的,还有鼓励人自学的。这是君子育人的五种方法。"

13.41 孟子曰:"大匠不为拙工改废绳墨,羿不为拙射变其彀率。君子引而不发,跃如也。中道而立,能者从之。"

《尽心上篇·41》节选

Mencius said, "A master craftsman would not change his tools just to make things easier for clumsy workers. Yi would not change his rules of archery for the sake of poor marksmen. A gentleman trains others in the way Yi taught archery. He drew bows without discharging the arrow, just to show his eagerness to shoot. When one stands in the right path, those who are capable enough will follow his example."

孟子说:"高明的工匠不因工人笨拙而改变或废弃规矩,羿也不因射手拙劣而改变拉弓的标准。君子育人就像教人射箭一样,拉满了弓,却不发箭,作出跃跃欲试的样子,自己站在正确的道路上,有能力的便会跟上来。"

13.42 孟子曰:"天下有道,以道殉身;天下无道,以身殉道;未闻以道殉乎人者也。"

《尽心上篇·42》

Mencius said, "When the rule of the empire is in order, a gentleman immerses himself in principles. When the rule of the state is in disorder, a gentleman will spare his own life to practice principles. I have never heard that a man could be spared at the expense of principles."

孟子说:"天下政治清明,道因之得以施行;天下政治黑暗,君子不惜为道而献身。没听说过可以牺牲道来迁就人的。"

13.45 孟子曰:"君子之于物也,爱之而弗仁;于民也,仁之而弗亲。亲亲而仁民,仁民而爱物。"

《尽心上篇·45》

Mencius said, "A gentleman needs to take good care of all things, but doesn't need to treat them with benevolence. He should treat people with benevolence only, and not with affection. A gentleman shows affection for his kin, benevolence toward other people and care for all other things."

孟子说:"君子对于物,只知道爱惜就够了,而不必以仁德对待它;对于百姓,只应以仁德对待他们而并不必表示亲爱。君子亲爱亲人,因而能仁爱百姓;仁爱百姓,因而能爱惜万物。"

十四、尽心下篇
Jin Xin, Part Two

《孟子》之第十四篇。孟子提出"春秋无义战","尽信书则不如无书","民为贵,社稷次之,君为轻"的观点。本篇共 38 章,节选其中 18 章。

孟子说:"天将降大任于是人也,必先苦其心志,劳其筋骨,饿其体肤,空乏其身,行拂乱其所为,动心忍性,曾益其所不能。"(《孟子·告子下》)

14.2　孟子曰:"春秋无义战。彼善于此,则有之矣。征者,上伐下也,敌国不相征也。"

《尽心下篇·2》

Mencius said, "There were no just wars in the Spring and Autumn Period. Only some kings were better than others, and senior states could send punitive expeditions against states of lower status, but states of the same status could not send punitive expeditions against one another."

孟子说:"春秋时代没有正义战争。有的君主比别个国家的君主好一些是有的。但征伐,只能是上级讨伐下级,同等级的国家是不能互相征伐的。所以说春秋无义战。"

14.3　孟子曰:"尽信书,则不如无书。吾于武成,取二三策而已矣。仁人无敌于天下,以至仁伐至不仁,而何其血之流杵也?"

《尽心下篇·3》

孟子所说的《书》指《尚书》，《武成》是书中一篇。在此篇中讲到周武王伐纣时有"血流漂杵"的记载，孟子很怀疑这记载的真实性。他认为以至仁伐至不仁，是不可能流那么多血的。所以他说"尽信书，则不如无书。"

Mencius said, "To believe unconditionally what the *Book of History* says is worse than if there were no *Book of History* in existence. I believe only a part of *Wu Cheng*. A benevolent man has no rival in the world. King Wu of Zhou was said to be benevolent, so how was it possible that in his campaign against the tyrant King Zhou of Shang so much blood was shed that twigs floated on it?"

Note: Wu Cheng is a chapter in the *Book of History*, in which it is recorded that "twigs floated on a river of blood" during King Wu of Zhou's expedition against King Zhou. Mencius doubted the truth of this record.

孟子说："完全相信《书》，则不如没有《书》。我对于《武成》篇中所说，只相信其中一部分内容罢了，对其余内容则持怀疑态度。仁人无敌于天下，以周武王这样至仁之人讨伐商纣王这样不仁的人，怎么会流那么多血，以至把木棒都漂了起来。"

◎ 尽心下篇 *Jin Xin, Part Two*

14.5 孟子曰:"梓匠轮舆能与人规矩,不能使人巧。"

《尽心下篇·5》

Mencius said, "A skilled craftsmen can pass on his techniques to others, but he cannot make others skillful."

孟子说:"高明的工匠可以把制作工艺传授与人,却不能使人具有高明的技巧。"

14.9 孟子曰:"身不行道,不行于妻子;使人不以道,不能行于妻子。"

《尽心下篇·9》

Mencius said, "If one does not behave according to principles one cannot expect one's wife and children to practice principles, not to mention other people. If one does not direct others according to principles, one cannot even direct one's wife and children, let alone others."

孟子说:"自己不依道而行,在妻子身上都行不通,更不要说对别人了。使唤人不合于道,连妻子也不能使唤,更不要说使唤别人了。"

14.10 孟子曰:"周于利者凶年不能杀,周于德者邪世不能乱。"

《尽心下篇·10》

Mencius said, "A wealthy man will not be poverty-stricken in famine years. A virtuous man will not be led astray during turbulent days."

孟子说:"财货富足的人荒年不受窘困,道德高尚的人乱世不会迷乱。"

14.12 孟子曰:"不信仁贤,则国空虚;无礼义,则上下乱;无政事,则财用不足。"

《尽心下篇·12》

Mencius said, "If virtuous and talented men are

not trusted, then the state will be devoid of all good men. If the rites are not observed, then the relations between superior and inferior will be in confusion. If a government is not properly administered, then the state's resources will fail."

孟子说:"不信任仁德贤能的人,国家就会无人;没有礼仪,上下关系就会混乱;没有好的政治,国家财政就会困难。"

14.13 孟子曰:"不仁而得国者,有之矣;不仁而得天下者,未之有也。"

《尽心下篇·13》

Mencius said, "A ruler who is not benevolent can hold onto a state. But no man who is not benevolent can rule the world."

孟子说:"不行仁道而能得到一国之政的,有这样的事;不行仁道而能得到天下的,这样的事却不曾有过。"

14.14 孟子曰:"民为贵,社稷次之,君为轻。是故得乎丘民而为天子,得乎天子为诸侯,得乎诸侯为大夫。诸侯危社稷,则变置。牺牲既成,粢盛既絜,祭祀以时,然而旱乾水溢,则变置社稷。"

《尽心下篇·14》

社稷:古代帝王、诸侯所祭的土神和谷神。人非土不立,非谷不食,故封土立社,示有土也;稷,五谷之长,故立稷而祭之。历代封建王朝必先立社稷坛。灭亡一个国家后,必先变置该国的社稷。因后多以社稷为国家政权的标志。絜:同"洁"。

Mencius said, "To a state, the people are the most important thing, the altars to the gods of earth and grain come second, and the ruler is the least important thing. He who wins the support of the people will become emperor, those who win the support of the emperor will become lords; those who win the support of their lord will become ministers. If a lord endangers the altars to the gods of earth and grain he should be replaced. Likewise, if sacrifices are offered according to the rites and on time but drought and floods persist, then the altars should be replaced. "

Note: In ancient times when a lord was granted territory, he set up an altar to the god of the earth to show that he possessed territory. Millet was the most important grain in ancient times, so altars to the god of millet were set up. When a state was annihilated, its altars to the gods of earth and millet were replaced. So the altars to the gods of earth and millet served as symbols of political power.

孟子说:"对一个国家来说,百姓最重要,社稷次之,君主为轻。所以得民心者便做天子,得天子心者便做诸侯,得诸侯心者便做大夫。诸侯危害国家,就要改立。依礼按时致祭,如还遭受水旱灾害,就要改立社稷。"

14.16 孟子曰:"仁也者,人也。合而言之,道也。"

《尽心下篇·16》

Mencius said,"To be benevolent is to be human. The joining of the two means principles."

孟子说:"仁的意思就是人,仁和人合在一起说,就是道。"

14.20 孟子曰:"贤者以其昭昭使人昭昭,今以其昏昏使人昭昭。"

《尽心下篇·20》

Mencius said, "Virtuous men, in instructing others, get themselves enlightened first, and then try to enlighten others with their enlightenment. But nowadays those who try to enlighten others are unenlightened themselves."

孟子说:"贤者教导别人必先使自己明白,然后才使别人明白;今为人师者,自己还不明白,却用这些模模糊糊的东西去使别人明白。"

14.21 孟子谓高子曰:"山径之蹊,间介然用之而成路;为间不用,则茅塞之矣。今茅塞子之心矣。"

《尽心下篇·21》

Mencius said to Gaozi, "A narrow mountain path will be broadened into a road if trodden frequently, but it will be overgrown with grass if not used for a long period of time. Now your mind is filled with grass."

孟子对高子说:"山间的小路只一点宽,经常有人走就会越来越宽。只要一段时间没人走,又会被野草堵塞了。现在野草也把你的心堵塞了。"

14.23 齐饥。陈臻曰:"国人皆以夫子将复为发棠,殆不可复。"孟子曰:"是为冯妇也。晋人有冯妇者,善搏虎,卒为善士。则之野,有众逐虎。虎负嵎,莫之敢撄。望见冯妇,趋而迎之。冯妇攘臂下车。众皆悦之。其为士者笑之。"

《尽心下篇·23》

棠：地名，故地在今山东省即墨县南八十里，当时是齐国仓廪所在地。冯妇：人名，姓冯，名妇，晋国人。

The State of Qi suffered from famine. Chen Zhen said to Mencius, "People believe that you will again ask the ruler of Qi to open the granaries at Tang to relieve the famine. But perhaps this will not be allowed?"

Mencius said, "If I do it again, I will be like Feng Fu, a man of the State of Jin who was famous for his skill at catching tigers. He later become an upright man and abandoned tiger hunting. Once he went out to the open country, where he saw a crowd of people chasing a tiger. The tiger was cornered at the foot of a hill. No one dared to go near it. On seeing Feng Fu, the people flocked round him. Feng Fu jumped down from his carriage, ready to catch the tiger. All were pleased, but scholars laughed at his behavior."

Note: Tang: Place name, in the south of present day Jimo County, Shandong Province. The granaries of the State of Qi were located there.

齐国遭了灾荒，陈臻对孟子说："人们都以为您会再次劝请齐王开仓赈灾的，您不会再这样做了吧。"

孟子说："再这样做便成了冯妇了。晋国有个人名叫冯妇，以打虎出名，后来变成善人声明不再打虎了。有一次他到野外，碰见许多人正追逐老虎。老虎被追至悬崖边，没有人敢靠近它。大家看见冯妇来，就迎上前去。冯妇也摩拳擦掌跳下车来。大家都很高兴，可是他的行动却受到士人的讥笑。"

14.24　孟子曰："口之于味也，目之于色也，耳之于声也，鼻之于臭也，四肢之于安佚也，性也，有命焉，君子不谓性也。仁之于父子也，义之于君臣也，礼之于宾主也，知之于贤者也，圣人之于天道也，命也，有性焉，君子不谓命也。"

《尽心下篇·24》

Mencius said, "It is human nature for the

mouth to desire delicious tastes, the eyes, beautiful colors, the ears, music, the nose, fragrant smells, and the four limbs, ease. But it is fate which decides whether one can obtain these. So gentlemen do no take these as their nature. It is fate which decides whether benevolence between fathers and sons, righteousness between sovereigns and ministers, decorum between hosts and guests, the wisdom of virtuous men and the principles of sages can be realized. But these are also part of human nature. So gentlemen do not take these things as being solely ruled by fate but aspire to realize them."

孟子说:"口对于美味,眼对于美色,耳对于好听的音乐,鼻对于香的气味,四肢对于舒服,这些爱好,都是天性,但是否能得到,却属于命运,所以君子不把这些认为是天性的必然,因此不去强求。仁在父子之间,义在君臣之间,礼在宾主之间,智慧在于贤者,圣人在于天道,是否能够实现,属于命运,但也是天性的必然,所以君子不把它们认为是该属于命运的,而努力求其实现。"

14.26 孟子曰:"逃墨必归于

杨,逃杨必归于儒。归,斯受之而已矣。今之与杨、墨辩者,如追放豚,既入其苙,又从而招之。"

《尽心下篇·26》

大概当时儒家中有以这种态度对待其它学派的人,而孟子对学生"往者不追"的态度正与此观点相反,所以孟子对这种思想加以批评。

Mencius said, "Those who desert the doctrines of Mozi are sure to accept the doctrines of Yangzi, and those who desert the doctrines of Yangzi are sure to return to the doctrines of Confucius. Once they have returned, we should accept them. But now, those who debate with disciples of those two schools are like people who chase stray pigs. Not only do they put the pigs back in the pigsty, they also tie their feet for fear they should stray again."

Note: It is possible that some followers of Confucius adopted such an attitude toward the followers of other schools. Mencius took the opposite attitude of "forgetting others' past misdeeds." So he criticized the above attitude.

孟子说:"离开墨子学派就会回到杨朱学派;离开杨朱学派的,一定会回到儒家来。只要回来,就接受他。今天有些同杨、墨两派辩论的人,好像追逐走失的猪一样,已经送回猪圈里,还要把它的脚绊住,生怕它再走失。"

14.28 孟子曰:"诸侯之宝三:土地,人民,政事。宝珠玉者,殃必及身。"

《尽心下篇·28》

Mencius said, "For the lords of the states there are three treasures: land, people and government. Those who value pearls and jade above these are sure to bring disaster on themselves."

孟子说:"诸侯有三宝:土地、百姓和政治。如果以珍珠美玉为宝,一定会祸及其身。"

14.31 孟子曰:"人皆有所不忍,达之于其所忍,仁也;人皆有所不为,达之于其所为,义也。人能充无欲害人之心，而仁不可胜用也；人能充无穿窬之心，而义不可胜用也；人能充无受尔汝之实，无所往而不为义也。士未可以言而言，是以言餂之也；可以言而不言，是以不言餂之也，是皆穿窬之类也。"

《尽心下篇·31》

Mencius said, "Everyone has something that he cannot bear. To extend such aversion to what he can bear is benevolence. Everyone has something that he refuses to do. To extend such aversion to what he is willing to do is righteousness. If one can fill his heart with aversion to hurting others, one's benevolence will be inexhaustible. If one fills one's heart with aversion to overstepping the mark, then his righteousness will be inexhaustible. If one fills one's heart with aversion to being despised by others, then one will be righteous wherever one goes. It is seeking profit by words if one comments when one should not comment. It is seeking profit by silence if one does not comment when one should comment. Both are equivalent to overstepping the mark."

孟子说:"每个人都有不忍心干的事,把这种心情扩充到所忍心干的事上,便是仁。每个人都有不肯干的事,把它扩充到所肯干的事上,便是义。人能够把不想害人之心扩而充之,仁便用不尽了。人能够把不偷窃的心扩而充之,义便用不尽了。人能够把不受人轻贱的言语行为扩而充之,那就无论到哪里都合于义了。譬如一个士人,对于不可以谈论的人而去谈论,这是用言语来引诱取利;对于可以谈论的人却不去谈论,这是用沉默来引诱取利,这都属偷窃一类的。"

14.32 孟子曰:"言近而指远者,善言也;守约而施博者,善道也。君子之言也,不下带而道存焉;君子之守,修其身而天下平。人病舍其田而芸人之田——所求于人者重,而所以自任者轻。"

《尽心下篇·32》

Mencius said, "Simple words with far-reaching meaning are good words. Principles easy to practice with good effects are good principles. Even when a gentleman talks about daily affairs, principles lie within his words. A gentleman begins with self-cultivation, but he can make the whole world peaceful. The trouble with some lies in neglecting their own fields but cultivating the fields of others—they are strict with others, but lenient with themselves."

孟子说:"言语浅近,意义却深远的,是善言;操作简单,效果却广大的,是善道。君子的言语,讲的虽是日常所见的事情,可'道'就在其中;君子的操守从修养自身开始,从而使天下太平。有些人的毛病在于放弃自己的田地,却去替别人耕田——要求别人严,对待自己宽。"

14.33 孟子曰:"尧舜,性者也;汤武,反之也。动容周旋中礼者,盛德之至也。哭死而哀,非为生者也。经德不回,非以干禄也。言语必信,非以正行也。君子行法，以俟命而已矣。"

《尽心下篇·33》

Mencius said, "Yao and Shun practiced benevolence and virtue out of their very natures. Tang and Wu returned to their natures after self-cultivation, and practiced benevolence and virtue. To behave and appear in accordance with the rites is the highest virtue. To mourn sorrowfully over the deceased is not done to impress the living. The purpose of acting according to the rites is not to seek office. The aim of speaking truth is not to show the correctness of one's actions. A gentleman will act according to the norms, but the result will be decided by Heaven."

孟子说："尧舜行仁德是出于本性；汤武是经过修身回复本性后力行。动作容貌完全合于礼的，是美德中最高的。哭死者而悲哀，不是故意做给活人看的。依据道德而行，不是为谋求官职。言语信实，不是为了表现自己的行为端正。君子处处依法度而行，结果如何，听天由命罢了。"

14.35 孟子曰:"养心莫善于寡欲。其为人也寡欲,虽有不存焉者,寡矣;其为人也多欲,虽有存焉者,寡矣。"

《尽心下篇·35》

Mencius said, "The best way to cultivate one's heart is to reduce one's desires. When one's desires are few, the merits that he loses will be few also. With numerous desires, one can hardly keep much goodness."

孟子说:"修养心性的方法最好是节制私欲。一个人少私欲,善性丧失就少;私欲多,其善性就不多了。"

图书在版编目（CIP）数据

《孟子》精华版 / 蔡希勤编著. —北京：华语教学出版社，2006
(中国圣人文化丛书)
ISBN 978－7－80200－219－7

Ⅰ.孟… Ⅱ.蔡… Ⅲ.汉语 － 对外汉语教学 － 语言读物 Ⅳ.H195.5

中国版本图书馆 CIP 数据核字（2006）第 072284 号

出版人：单 瑛
责任编辑：韩芙芸　　封面设计：唐少文
印刷监制：佟汉冬　　插图绘制：李士伋

《孟子》精华版
蔡希勤 编注
*

©华语教学出版社
华语教学出版社出版
（中国北京百万庄大街 24 号　邮政编码 100037）
电话: 010-68320585 传真: 010-68326333
网址：www.sinolingua.com.cn
电子信箱:hyjx@sinolingua.com.cn
北京外文印刷厂印刷
中国国际图书贸易总公司海外发行
（中国北京车公庄西路 35 号）
北京邮政信箱第 399 号　邮政编码 100044
新华书店国内发行
2006 年（大 32 开）第一版
2007 年第二次印刷
（汉英）
ISBN 978－7－80200－219－7
9－CE－3736P
定价：38.80 元